A PRACTICAL GUIDE TO TORAH LEARNING

A PRACTICAL GUIDE TO TORAH LEARNING

Dovid Landesman

JASON ARONSON INC.
Northvale, New Jersey
London

This book was set in 11 pt. Bembo
by Kelby and Teresa Bowers, Compublishing of Cincinnati, Ohio,

10 9 8 7 6 5 4 3 2 1

Library of Congress Cataloging-in-Publication Data

Landesman, Dovid.
A practical guide to Torah learning / Dovid Landesman.
p. cm.
Includes bibliographical references and index.
ISBN 1–56821–320–4
1.Talmud—Introductions. 2.Talmud—Hermeneutics. 3.Jewish law—Interpretation and construction. 4.Rabbinical literature—History and criticism. I.Title.
BM 503.5.L36 1995
296.1'07—dc20 94–32902

Manufactured in the United States of America. Jason Aronson Inc. offers books and cassettes. For information and catalog write to Jason Aronson Inc., 230 Livingston Street, Northvale, New Jersey 07647.

Contents

Preface

במקום שאין אנשים השתדל להיות איש (אבות ב:ו)

The very title of this work is somewhat pretentious, for it would seem to suggest that the author is qualified to serve as a guide through the vast sea of Jewish learning. I therefore decided to qualify the title by adding the word practical, for it is my intention to provide the reader with a basic reference work—rather than a thorough guide—that will hopefully be of some use in his studies.

This book has its roots in my own experiences when I began learning in yeshivah. My teachers presupposed a great deal of knowledge on my part—perhaps justifiably—and I was embarrassed to ask what I thought were *klotz kashyas*—foolish questions that would reveal my ignorance. I remember my frustrations in trying to find a *halachah* that they had quoted from the Rambam, frustrations brought about by my total unfamiliarity with the system that the Rambam had used to categorize his work.

I also was totally incapable of placing works into any kind of historical context or perspective. I assumed, for example, that the Mordechai must be relatively unimportant since his commentary was printed in small letters at the very end of the Talmud. Additionally, I had no inkling of the existence of a well-defined structure of development, both in halachic literature and in the Talmud itself.

When my children began their studies in yeshivah, I sensed that my own shortcomings as a student were about to be repeated, for no one was really teaching them how to use *seforim*. Moreover, when reviewing what they had learned in the classroom—an exercise in parenting that I pray has left no permanent scars—I found that while they were quite capable of repeating what the *rebbi* had taught them, they had little idea of what the *sugya* was really all about. Again, it was not their fault, for no one had ever tried to explain the dynamics of the talmudic dialogue to them. My efforts to do so were not entirely successful, for they rightfully complained that "the *rebbi* didn't teach it that way."

Through the years, I made notes on various topics and even committed some of them into my computer's memory. The idea of publishing them as a book began to germinate in my mind, and I reviewed the material trying to establish a structure for it. I thought that I knew what I wanted to include, but now that the work is ready for publication, I'm not certain that I've accomplished all that I set out to do. In order not to reach the point of having to make value judgments vis-à-vis authors to be included and those who are not mentioned, I decided—for the most part—to limit myself to those works appended to the texts that the student will probably use in the classroom or *beis midrash,* adding the classic commentators whose works are widely quoted in the course of a lecture. This system is unquestionably faulty—how can one talk about the *Yad ha-Chazakah* without mentioning R. Chaim Soloveitchik or the *Or Somayach*! Nevertheless, the line had to be drawn somewhere, even if the decision was arbitrary.

The first section of this work relates to the literature of the Talmud. It begins with a general outline of the presentation of the Talmud meant for those just beginning their studies. It proceeds to examine the various commentaries usually printed alongside the Talmud, offering a brief paragraph or two about the author. Again, I apologize to the reader about the arbitrariness of my decisions about what to include about each commentator.

The second section parallels the first but deals with the literature of *halachah,* covering the era of the *geonim* through the contemporary period. The presentation is somewhat more elaborate in this section, for experience has shown that most students are less familiar with the issues and authors with which this section deals.

The third section includes those works that are not included in the Talmud or in the halachic codes, but that are an integral part of the development of both the Talmud and halachic literature. The last chapter of this section provides a brief overview of some of the philosophic and ethical literature that the student will likely come across in his first years of study.

The fourth section deals with the structure of the Talmud itself and is meant to provide the reader with a guide to understanding the how and why of talmudic dialogue. The first two chapters are based on research undertaken in cooperation with R. Nathan Lopez Cardozo of Jerusalem—author of *The Infinite Chain*—and I am grateful for his kind permission to include it in this work. Chapter 20, which analyzes one of the most familiar talmudic dialogues, is meant to give the reader a picture of how the Talmud resolves a question as well as showing the student how the comments of the *rishonim* and *acharonim* can be used to enhance their comprehension.

I often asked my children—and students—why they thought that Rashi or Tosafos made a comment that seems to be unrelated to explaining the dialogue itself. I pray that the analysis in chapter 20 will help students answer that question on their own in other situations by showing them how to look at the structure of a *sugya* as a whole.

Originally, I thought of including a brief lexicon of talmudic terminology and concepts, but a number of excellent recent publications have made this unnecessary. The glossary includes those Hebrew terms that are transliterated in this work. Many of the entries have been expanded to explain concepts that the student will encounter in the course of his studies. The appendices included are meant to provide the student with basic reference materials. The index is designed to help the student quickly find a reference to a name or *sefer*. To avoid confusion, I have used the common dating system throughout this work. The parallel Hebrew year can be established by adding 3760.

I would like to express my sincere appreciation to Mr. Arthur Kurzweil of Jason Aronson Inc., who has given me license to follow my own instincts regarding the direction of this work. It is a privilege to be associated with Reb Avrohom and his firm, for their commitment to the publication of serious Torah literature is truly worthy of commendation.

Publication of this work would not have been possible had God not granted me the opportunity to study under a number of rebbis who were masters in helping me learn how to learn. Although they suffered in their attempts to teach me, I pray that this book will give them some long-overdue *nachas* and prove that יש תקוה לאחריתך. Nor would this work have been possible without His gift of parents—Mr. and Mrs. Louis Landesman of Jerusalem—who were prepared to undertake considerable emotional and financial sacrifice to enable me to leave home and study in yeshivah. This gift was later expanded by His provision of in-laws—Rabbi and Mrs. Yitzchok Chinn of McKeesport, Pennsylvania—whose greatest source of pride is in having realized the fulfillment of the verse *And all your children shall be learned.*

This work is dedicated to my wife and children in appreciation for their encouragement and support. May God grant that we be found worthy to share in His abundant grace and together welcome the coming of *Mashiach,* speedily and in our days.

Dovid Landesman
Kfar Chassidim

I

TALMUDIC LITERATURE

To most of us, the term Talmud is synonymous with the Babylonian Talmud, i.e., the discussions of the *mishnayos* by the *tanna'im* and *amora'im* who studied and taught in the yeshivos of Eretz Yisrael and the major Babylonian academies of Nehardea, Sura, Pumbedisa, Masa Mechasya, and Mechoza. Although we refer to it as the Talmud *Bavli,* there are numerous examples within the folios of discussions of the academies of Eretz Yisrael and of *tanna'im* and *amora'im* who spent their entire lives there. Additionally, we often find records of *amora'im* who traveled between the academies of Bavel and Eretz Yisrael and of correspondence between the two centers of Jewry. However, with the beginning of the era of the *amora'im,* the yeshivos of Bavel assumed ascendancy. It should be noted that there were academies in Bavel from the very beginning of the era of the *tanna'im*. Hillel, for example, came from Bavel to study in Eretz Yisrael. Rav (Abba Aricha), the first of the *amora'im,* was born in Bavel and accompanied his uncle R.Chiyah to study under R.Yehudah ha-Nasi. He only rejoined his colleague Shmuel in Bavel well after his master's death.

While it is beyond the scope of this work to offer the reader an analysis of the differences between the Talmud *Bavli* and the *Yerushalmi,* it should be noted that the Talmud *Bavli* is usually considered to be a firmer base for *halachah* in that its editing took place over a longer period of time and, more importantly, because the academies in Bavel—and the Babylonian Jewish community as a whole—were less subject to outside interferences.

The sample of the text on page 5 is representative of what has become the traditional presentation of the Babylonian Talmud. The folio chosen (*Bava Metzia* 11a) is a reproduction from the Romm Talmud, printed in Vilna in 1886. This edition has become the standard for all subsequent editions vis–à–vis layout and major materials included on the page. The reader may find minor additions included along the margins of subsequent editions.

The layout of the page provides us with the following information. Along the top, the name of the chapter is followed by its number and the name of the tractate. The left margin has the number of the folio; the number is signified by the corresponding Hebrew letter (יא having the value of 11). On the reverse side of this folio, the number appears in Arabic numerals in the upper right-hand corner. In this case, the number is 22 since it is the twenty-second page of the tractate. The folio of the Talmud with the Hebrew letter in the top left-hand corner is referred to as עמוד א—side a—while the side of the page with the Arabic numeral in the right-hand corner is referred to as עמוד ב—side b. Traditionally, all tractates in the Babylonian Talmud begin from the letter ב, i.e., page two.

The middle of the page contains the text of the Talmud printed in square Hebrew script. The page in our example begins with text from the Talmud that is then followed by a *mishnah*. The introduction of a new *mishnah* is indicated by the Hebrew letters מתני׳—an abbreviated form of the word מתניתין, which is the Aramaic term for the Mishnah. *Mishnayos* quoted at the beginning of a chapter are not preceded by the letters מתני׳. The division of the Mishnah cited in the Talmud

ילפינן מציאה מגט ומר סבר לא ילפינן מציאה מגט ואיבעית אימא בקטנה כולי עלמא לא פליגי דילפינן מציאה מגט והכא בקטן קא מיפלגי מר סבר ילפינן קטן מקטנה ומר סבר לא ילפינן קטן מקטנה ואיבעית אימא מר אמר הדא ומר אמר הדא ולא פליגי:

מתני' ראה אותן רצין אחר מציאה אחר צבי שבור אחר גוזלות שלא פרחו ואמר זכתה לי שדי זכתה לו היה צבי רץ כדרכו או שהיו גוזלות מפריחין ואמר זכתה לי שדי לא אמר כלום:

גמ' אמר רב יהודה אמר שמואל והוא שעומד בצד שדהו ותקני ליה שדהו דאמר ר' יוסי בר' חנינא חצרו של אדם קונה לו שלא מדעתו דני מילי בחצר המשתמרת אבל חצר שאינה משתמרת אי עומד בצד שדהו אין אי לא לא ומנא תימרא דחצר שאינה משתמרת אי עומד בצד שדהו אין אי לא לא דתניא היה עומד בעיר ואומר יודע אני שעומר שיש לי בשדה פועלים שכחוהו לא יהא שכחה יכול לא יהא שכחה תלמוד לומר ושכחת עומר בשדה בשדה ושכחת ולא בעיר הא גופא קשיא אמרת יכול לא יהא שכחה אלמא הוי שכחה תסיב לה נמרא בשדה ושכחת ולא בעיר אלמא לא הוי שכחה אלא לאו הכי קאמר בשדה שכוח מעיקרו הוי שכחה זכור ולבסוף שכוח אין שכחה מאי טעמא דכיון דקאי גבה הויא ליה חצרו וזכתה ליה אבל בעיר אפילו זכור ולבסוף שכוח הויא שכחה מאי טעמא דליתיה גביה דלזכי ליה ממאי דלמא גזירת הכתוב היא דבשדה נהוי שכחה ובעיר לא נהוי שכחה אמר קרא לא תשוב לקחתו לרבות שכחת העיר האי מבעי ליה ללאו אם כן נימא קרא לא תקחנו מאי לא תשוב לרבות שכחת העיר ואכתי מבעי ליה לכדתנן שלפניו אין שכחה שלאחריו יש שכחה שהוא בבל תשוב זה הכלל כל שהוא בבל תשוב שכחה כל שאינו בבל תשוב אינו שכחה אמר רב אשי אמר קרא והיה לרבות שכחת העיר וכן אמר עולא והוא שעומד בצד שדהו וכן אמר רבה בר בר חנה והוא שעומד בצד שדהו איתיביה רבי אבא לעולא מעשה ברבן גמליאל וזקנים שהיו באים בספינה אמר רבן גמליאל עישור שאני עתיד למוד נתון ליהושע ומקומו

sometimes differs in length from that cited in volumes of the Mishnah alone. The beginning of the talmudic discussion of the Mishnah is indicated by the Hebrew letters גמ׳—an abbreviation of the word גמרא, the Aramaic term for the Talmud.

Within the text of the Talmud, the following points should be taken into account. When the Talmud offers a comparison with another source, either as support for an opinion or to pose a question, it often precedes the quotation by using the term תנן—we learned— if the other source is a *mishnah,* or by using the similar term תניא if the second source is a *beraisa.* The prefatory remark תנא is used when the source is a *tosefta.* תא שמע—come and hear—can refer to either a *mishnah,* a *beraisa,* or a *tosefta.*

The material included on each page was first set in the Bromberg edition of the Talmud (Venice 1519–1523) and all subsequent editions have followed this format. It should be noted that earlier editions varied vis–à–vis the amount of material on each page. The Munich manuscript (14th century), the oldest complete version of the Talmud extant, has major differences as regards the beginning and end of each page. It would seem that once the Bromberg edition—which was the first complete printed version of the Talmud—was published, a consensus was reached to adhere to this format so as to create a standard version for reference purposes.

The Bromberg edition also established the practice of placing the commentary of Rashi on the inside margin of each page and the commentary of the Tosafos on the outside margin. Additionally, the practice of placing four lines of Rashi and Tosafos above the beginning of the talmudic text also dates from this edition.

The text of the Talmud itself is based on Rashi's editing of the manuscripts available to him. This editing was necessary because, before the invention of the printing press, all editions of the Talmud were handwritten and copied, and errors were quite common. The changes that Rashi made in his text are often the subject of the comments of

Tosafos, and there are numerous instances where we find the latter defending the original texts that Rashi emended. Changes to the text were also made by the Maharshal and the Maharsha. As we shall see, other editorial suggestions were made by both the Bach and the Gra; however, their changes were not included within the text but were added as glosses on the margins.

Within the text of the Talmud, one often finds words in parentheses and/or in brackets. The former represent suggestions that the enclosed text be omitted, whereas the latter are suggestions for text that should be included. In many cases, explanations for these suggestions have been included by the publishers in the margins.

The text of the Romm edition is based on censored editions—most likely that printed in Basle in 1578–1581—and we find numerous instances where the censors changed words or phrases or deleted entire sentences and paragraphs. References to the early Christians and to the founder of the church were often deleted by the publishers or changed. It should be noted that the printing industry was controlled by the church and/or state, and all manuscripts were subject to review before publication. Some of these changes were forced, whereas others were voluntarily made by Jewish publishers anxious to maintain harmonious relations.

The Munich manuscript includes the texts that were censored from the Vilna edition. The *Ein Yaakov* compilation of the *aggados* of the Talmud also includes many of the censored texts as well as minor differences from the parallel texts in the Vilna edition. It would seem that the *Ein Yaakov* was based on the Salonika edition of the Talmud that was printed shortly after the Bromberg edition but was not subject to the same heavy censorship as were editions published in Western Europe. This might also account for the discrepancies between the text of Rashi printed in the *Ein Yaakov* and that printed in the Vilna edition.

1

Commentaries That Appear Alongside the Text

The Babylonian Talmud, from its very first printing, has had a number of commentaries and notes included on each page. Although there are minor variations among editions published in different countries and at different times, the Romm Vilna edition has become the standard, as we have already noted. That edition includes the following:

1.1 Rashi

On the inside margin of the page is the commentary of Rashi (R. Shlomo Yitzchaki, France — 1040–1105). Rashi, the most famous of the commentators to the Talmud, explains and translates the talmudic dialogue while, for the most part, refraining from subjecting the text to analysis or comparison to parallel texts in other tractates. The commentary can be seen as a phraseological exposition designed to enable the student to understand the discussion. Rashi provides a wealth of historical and practical information that gives the student the means to understand the references to places and things with which most readers would be unfamiliar. In addition, he often translates obscure terminology into Old French—preceded by the comment לע״ז.

Rashi edited his commentary extensively; the commentary that appears in our texts is, according to tradition, the third version. His commentary has become so popular that no edition of the Talmud can be considered complete without its inclusion. According to tradition, Rashi wrote a commentary to the entire Talmud, but did not manage to complete the editing process before he passed away. The commentary that apppears in his name to tractate *Nedarim* is not considered to be his. The commentary to tractate *Makkos* (from 19b) was completed by his student and son-in-law, R. Yehudah ben Nasan (Rivan) and the commentary to tractate *Bava Basra* (from 29a) was written in his style by his grandson, R. Shmuel ben Meir (Rashbam). The commentary of Rashi that is usually printed alongside the Rif is not considered to be accurate and may be based on earlier versions. Some editions of the Talmud have the headwords of Rashi's commentary set in bold, square Hebrew script.

1.2 *Tosafos*

The word *tosafos*—additions—indicates that the commentary was meant as an addition to that of Rashi. Unlike the commentary of Rashi, the commentary of the Tosafos is more extensive, often serving as an extension to the talmudic dialogue itself. In many instances, we find the Tosafos quoting parallel texts so as to reconcile apparent contradictions. In addition, the commentary of the Tosafos offers alternative explanations to those offered by Rashi and questions the basis for Rashi's textual emendations. When quoting Rashi, the Tosafos often refers to the commentary as פירוש בקונטרס—it was explained in the pamphlet. It would appear that this is based on the fact that Rashi's commentary was copied into booklets that were studied alongside the handcopied editions of the Talmud.

The commentary of the Tosafos that appears in our editions was written primarily by a group of scholars in France and Germany in the twelfth and thirteenth centuries. Many of these scholars were members of Rashi's family. Among them we find:

Rivan, R. Yehudah ben Nasan; and *Ram,* R. Meir ben Shmuel—Rashi's sons-in-law
Rashbam, R. Shmuel ben Meir; and *Rabbenu Tam,* R. Yaakov ben Meir—Rashi's grandsons
Ri, R. Yitzchak of Dampierre—Rashi's great-grandson

Other scholars whose comments are included in the commentary of Tosafos include Rabbenu Chaim, Rabbenu Peretz, R. Meir of Ruttenberg (*Maharam*), Rabbenu Shimon and R. Moshe of Coucy (author of the *Semag*). The period of activity of the Tosafos was approximately 200 years and included schools of study in northern and southern France, England, Germany, and Italy.

The Tosafos printed alongside most of the tractates of the Talmud in the Vilna edition is referred to as Tosafos Tuch (Touques), after the French city where the commentary was edited.

Other editions of the Tosafos were prepared elsewhere and are sometimes included in the Talmud under the title *Tosafos Yeshanim.*

1.3 *Rabbenu Chananel*

In many of the tractates of the Talmud, the commentary of Rabbenu Chananel ben Chushiel (Kirouan, North Africa—11th century) is included on the outside margin. Unlike the commentaries of Rashi and Tosafos, the commentary of Rabbenu Chananel is a synopsis of the talmudic discussion and does not explain the text or compare it to other sources. The commentary of Rabbenu Chananel to the entire Talmud is not extant. In some tractates the commentary of Rabbenu Nissim *Gaon* (North Africa—11th century) or variant *tosafos* are offered instead or as well.

1.4 *Ein Mishpat Ner Mitzvah*

Compiled by R.Yehoshua Boaz (Italy—16th century), the *Ein Mishpat* provides source references to enable the student to find the relevant citations in halachic literature and is found on the outside margin of the page. The author added a square Hebrew letter printed in superscript to the text of the Talmud to indicate his notation and usually cites three primary sources:

Yad ha-Chazakah—by the Rambam—abbreviated as מיי׳. The chapter is abbreviated as פ׳ for פרק, followed by the number of the chapter, its halachic subject, and subsection number.

Sefer Mitzvos Gadol—by R. Moshe of Coucy—abbreviated as סמ״ג. The citation refers to either positive or negative commandments according to which that work is divided, followed by the relevant number.

Tur Shulchan Aruch—by R.Yaakov ben Asher—abbreviated as טוש״ע. The author notes the division in which the source can be found—או״ח referring to *Orach Chaim,* אה״ע referring to *Even ha-Ezer,* י״ד referring to *Yoreh De'ah,* and ח״מ referring to *Choshen Mishpat.* This is followed by the chapter number and subsection. References to the *Shulchan Aruch* itself are not cited since that work follows the order of the *Tur,* although the subsection number refers to the paragraph divisions introduced in the *Shulchan Aruch.*

In the first comment of the *Ein Mishpat* on the opposite page, we find the following notations:

מיי׳ פי״ז מהלכות אבידה הל׳ י, ופ״ד מהל׳ זכייה ומתנה הל׳ ט וע׳ בהשגות ובמ״מ—This refers us to the Rambam's *Yad ha-Chazakah,* chapter 17 of the laws of found property, paragraph 10, and to an additional reference to chapter 4 of the laws of acquisition and gifts, paragraph 9. The reader is also referred to the glosses of the Ra'avad to the Rambam—noted as השגות—and to the commentary of the *Mishneh la-Melech*—abbreviated as מ״מ.

ילפינן מציאה מגט ומר סבר לא ילפינן מציאה מגט ואיבעית אימא בקטנה כולי עלמא לא פליגי דילפינן מציאה מגט והכא בקטן קא מיפלגי מר סבר ילפינן קטן מקטנה ומר סבר לא ילפינן קטן מקטנה ואיבעית אימא מר אמר הדא ומר אמר הדא ולא פליגי:

מתני' ראה אותן רצין אחר מציאה אחר צבי שבור אחר גוזלות שלא פרחו ואמר זכתה לי שדי זכתה לו היה צבי רץ כדרכו או שהיו גוזלות מפריחין ואמר זכתה לי שדי לא אמר כלום:

גמ' אמר רב יהודה אמר שמואל והוא שעומד בצד שדהו ותקני ליה שדהו דאמר ר' יוסי בר' חנינא חצרו של אדם קונה לו שלא מדעתו תני מילי בחצר המשתמרת אבל חצר שאינה משתמרת אי עומד בצד שדהו אין אי לא לא ומנא תימרא דחצר שאינה משתמרת אי עומד בצד שדהו אין אי לא לא דתניא היה עומד בעיר ואומר יודע אני שעומר שיש לי בשדה פועלים שכחוהו לא יהא שכחה יכול לא יהא שכחה תלמוד לומר ושכחת עומר בשדה בשדה ושכחת ולא בעיר הא גופא קשיא אמרת יכול לא יהא שכחה אלמא הוי שכחה תנסב לה גמרא בשדה ושכחת ולא בעיר אלמא לא הוי שכחה אלא לאו הכי קאמר בשדה שכוח מעיקרו הוי שכחה זכור ולבסוף שכוח אין שכחה מאי טעמא דכיון דקאי גביה הויא ליה חצרו וזכתה ליה אבל בעיר אפילו זכור ולבסוף שכוח הויא שכחה מאי טעמא דליתיה גביה דלזכי ליה ממאי דלמא גזירת הכתוב היא דבשדה נהוי שכחה ובעיר לא נהוי שכחה אמר קרא לא תשוב לקחתו לרבות שכחת העיר האי מיבעי ליה ללאו אם כן נימא קרא לא תקחנו מאי לא תשוב לרבות שכחת העיר ואכתי מיבעי ליה לכדתנן שלפניו אין שכחה שלאחריו יש שכחה שהוא בבל תשוב זה הכלל כל שהוא בבל תשוב שכחה כל שאינו בבל תשוב אינו שכחה אמר רב אשי אמר קרא והיה לרבות שכחת העיר וכן אמר עולא והוא שעומד בצד שדהו וכן אמר רבה בר בר חנה והוא שעומד בצד שדהו איתיביה רבי אבא לעולא מעשה ברבן גמליאל וזקנים שהיו באים בספינה אמר רבן גמליאל עישור שאני עתיד למוד נתון ליהושע ומקומו

רש"י

ילפיק מגילה מגט. כי היכי דגבי גט אית לה חצר לקטנה גבי מציאה נמי אית לה: ומר סבר לא ילפיק. משנה מאוסרת וגבי מציאה חצר מאם המלא אתרבאי וליכא למימר דמציאות תהא משום דאין עליה לדבר עבירה דאצטריך למכתב התם: והכא בקטן פליגי. דלא אשכחן דגבי גיה חצר: הדא ומר אמר חדא כו'. ר"ש בן לקיש אמר לענין מציאה ורבי יוחנן לענין גט ולא נגד מר אמר קטן ומר אמר קטנה: **מתני'** אחר צבי שבור. דהוה הזמינה דמציאה שאינו יכול לרוץ ומשתמר בתוך השדה אם לא ישלטו אחרים: **גמ'** או עומד בצד שדהו אין. דשכשיו היא משתמרת על ידו: עומר שיש לי בשדה. שהנחתיו שם מדעתי וסמכתי על הפועלים שיביאוהו ופועלים שכחוהו: לא יהא שכחה. אם חזר ושכחו: בשדה ושכחת. אם שכחתו בהולך מן השדה הוי שכחה ולא ששכחתו משנכנסת לעיר: אלא לאו הכי קאמר בשדה שכוח מעיקרו כו'. כגון הלוקט בשדה שומר השכוח מעיקרו ששכחו האי תחילה נשעל הוי שכחה אבל זכור שאיתו שם מדעתו ולבסוף שכחו על ידי פועלים לא הוי שכחה: אבל בעיר. משנכנס לעיר אפילו זכור ולבסוף שכח הוי שכחה דליתיה גביה כו' והכי קא נסיב ליה תנא לתלמודיה יכול לא יהא שכחה ת"ל בשדה ושכחת כשעודך בשדה הוא דבעינן דשכחתיה אתה ולא בעיר לא בעינן ושכחת שאף שכחת פועלים עושה אותה שכחה: וממאי. דקרא הכי מתרץ ומתני' הכי אמרה: דלמא גזירת הכתוב היא. דמשמע דבשדה יהא שכחה אבל משבא בעל הבית לעיר אין שכחתו ושכחת פועלים כלום והכי קאמר יכול יהא שכחה ת"ל כו': שלפניו אין שכחה. בשעת הקצר קאי יחד שהתחיל לקצור מראש השורה ושכח לפניו ולאחריו שלאחריו הוי שכחה שלפניו לא הוי שכחה: והיה. לגר ליתום ולאלמנה יהיה: עישור שאני עתיד למוד. מכר שלא עישר מפירותיו והוקשה לו ומיהר למעשר כאשר הוא שם: נתון ליהושע. לרבי יהושע בן חנניה שהיה עמו בספינה והוא לוי ונוטל מעשר ראשון כדאמרי' בערכין (דף יא:) מעשה ברבי יהושע שהלך לסייע את ר' יוחנן בן גודגדא בהגפת דלתות אמר לו חזור בך שאתה מן המשוררים ואני מן המשוערים והמשורר שסייע במיתה:

תוספות

ילפינן מגילה מגט. הא ילפיק הי מדרבנן ומגילות קטן לא הוי אלא מדרבנן אפילו לרבי יוסי דאמר (לקמן דף יב) גזל גמור הויא מדבריהם ולענין יד לא פליגי דילפיק אלא לענין חצר:

זכתה לו. [א] נראה אע"ג דלא אמר זכתה לי דחכמה לו כדאמרי' לעיל (דף י.) לא תקון רבנן דלקני כי לא אמר מאי הוי והא לא שמר דהכא היינו משום דנפל לו עליה דגלי בדעתיה שרוצה לקנות אבל הכא מי יימר דרוצה לקנות והדרכה משמע לעיל דאי לא נפל קנה נמי ואע"ג דלא אמר תיקני ועוד דאמר רבי יוסי בר' חנינא חצרו של אדם קונה לו שלא מדעתו אלמא אע"ג דלא אמר קני והכא נקט משום סיפא דאפילו אמר כיון דרץ כדרכו לא קני:

היה צבי רץ כדרכו. כ"ה אפי' גבי שבור אם רץ אחריו ואין מגיעו אלא אורחא דמילתא נקט דשבור כדרכו אין מגיעו:

הא במשתמרת כו'. במאי דתנן שור שנגח את הפרה (ב"ק דף מט: ושם ד"ה והלכתא) אמר משכטו של גר כיון ישראל ומת הגר כו' זה קונה השאר כו' ופריך ותקני ליה חצרו דאמר ר' יוסי בר' חנינא כו' ומסיק דליתיה פי' למטה בחצרו וקשה דהתם משמע דהוי בחצר המשתמרת מדמייתי עלה מרבי יוסי בר' חנינא ומיירי במשתמרת כדשכת הכא ועוד דמסתמא ביתו דהוא משתמר הוא שמשם שם המשכון וא"כ כי ליתיה נמי לקני ועוד דהפריך ליה מדרבי יוסי בר' חנינא לפרוך ממתני' ומיהו זה טעם לתרץ דמתני' הי משום דנתכוין לאסיר כה ואמר וכתה לי לכך מייתי מרבי יוסי בר' חנינא [ב] וי"ל דה"ה דליתיה למשכון בחצר אבל מטה גם לפי המקנן מיירי דליתיה בחצר ולכך לא פריך ממתני' כ"א מרבי יוסי בר' חנינא וה"ה פרק הזורק (גיטין דף עז: ושם ד"ה ושם) דתנן זרק לתוך ביתה או לתוך חצרה מגורשת משמע דמשתמרת ואפילו הכי קאמר שלא והוא שעומדת בצד ביתה וי"ל דדוקא גבי גט דאיתיה בעל כרחה בעינן שעומדת בצד ביתה כדאמר במתניתין:

זכור ולבסוף שכוח. פירוש זכור בשעה שהשכחה מתחלת שכבר שכחוהו פועלים ולבסוף שכח גם הוא ושכוח מעיקרו הוי כששכחו הפועלים שכח גם הוא אבל מה שהוא זכור בשעה שהפועלים זוכרין אין זה זכור ולבסוף שכוח דא"כ לא תמצא שכחה לעולם דכששדהו מלאה עומרין יאמר יזכה לי שדי:

דלמא גזירת הכתוב היא. פרש"י ועגרום יכול יהא שכחה ותימה לפי שרוצה לסתור ראייתו מניה הברייתא ועוד מה מפרך לרבות שכחת העיר והלא בברייתא יליף דזכור ולבסוף שכוח לא הוי שכחה דקתני יודע אני שפועלים שכחוהו והכא דדריש לרבות שכחת העיר יעמיד בשכוח מעיקרא לכך י"ל שאינו סותר ראייתו אלא גמרא קשה לו על הברייתא מנ"ל למדרש מיעוטא על דיוקא דקרא דדריש בשדה ושכחת דהייט שכוח מעיקרא אבל זכור ולבסוף שכוח לא הוי שכחה ועל זה קאי מיעוטא למר דבעיר אפילו זכור ולבסוף שכוח הוי שכחה דלמא גזירת הכתוב היא ובשדה הוי שכחה שכוח מעיקרא ולא בעיר והכי מסתברא טפי לאוקמי מיעוט אצופיה דקרא בשדה ושכחת ולא בעיר והשתא תשני שפיר לרבות שכחת העיר ועל"ל מי קאי אפשטיה דקרא: **זה** הכלל. לאתויי קמן אים:

עישור שאני עתיד למוד. פרש"י פרק קמא דקידושין (דף כו: ושם ד"ה מעשר) שהיה ירא פן יאמתו עליו בני ביתו שעישר ויאכלו טבל דחזקה על חבר שאינו מוציא מתחת ידו דבר שאינו מתוקן וקשה דהיינו דוקא כשבר שמת או כהולך ואין בדעתו לשוב עד ימים רבים ...

סמ"ג עשין סי' ע"ד—This refers us to *Sefer Mitzvos Gadol,* positive precepts, number 74.

טוש"ע ח"מ סי' רסח סעיף ה וסי' רמג סעיף כג—This refers us to *Tur Shulchan Aruch,* division *Choshen Mishpat,* chapter 268, paragraph 5, with an additional reference to chapter 243, paragraph 23.

R. Yehoshua Boaz intended to add a commentary to his work, which accounts for the large letters next to the notation, but he did not complete it.

1.5 *Torah Or*

Also compiled by R. Yehoshua Boaz, *Torah Or* is found in the margin between the text of the Talmud and the commentaries of Rashi and Tosafos, and provides the scriptural source for verses cited in the Talmud. The author added a superscript ^{o} as a symbol for his notation.

1.6 *Masores ha-Shas*

These references are usually found in the inside margin, although when space requirements did not allow for this, they can be found under the author's *Ein Mishpat. Masores ha-Shas* provides the student with the appropriate reference for materials cited from other tractates, suggestions for alternative readings—usually preceded by the comment צ"ל—צריך לומר (it should be said)—as well as explanations of terms (primarily quoted from the *Aruch*). Citations from other tractates include the name of the tractate and the folio—a period after the folio number indicating side a and a colon indicating side b. Cross-references to sources within the same tractate are noted by the word לעיל—previously—or לקמן—later. The author does not necessarily cite all cross-references; at times the student will find a reference followed by the abbreviation וש"נ—ושם נסמן (there it has been noted), indicating that other cross-references are offered at the source cited.

Masores ha-Shas was first compiled by R. Yehoshua Boaz and was reedited by R. Yishayahu Pick (see 4:7). The additions of the latter are indicated by square brackets. The authors noted their comments with an asterisk in the text.

1.7 *ha-Gaos ha-Bach*

Compiled by R. Yoel Sirkes (see 10.2), the *ha-Gaos ha-Bach* are the suggestions for textual emendations in the Talmud and Rashi copied from the notes that the author added to his copy of the Talmud. The Bach noted his comments to the text by enclosing a letter in Rashi script within parentheses.

1.8 *ha-Gaos ha-Gra*

Similar in content to *ha-Gaos ha-Bach, ha-Gaos ha-Gra* are the suggestions for emendations that R. Eliyahu, the *Gaon* of Vilna (see 11.14) wrote in the margins of his copy of the Talmud. The comments are noted within the text by use of a square Hebrew letter within square brackets.

1.9 *Gilyon ha-Shas*

The terse and sometimes cryptic comments to the text of the Talmud, or to the commentaries of Rashi and Tosafos, of R. Akiva Eiger (see 3.10). The author sometimes offers a reference to a similar source within the Talmud that differs only slightly from that in the text. Usually, however, he cites another source that either contradicts or poses a difficulty to the subject under discussion. Rarely, the author provides the answer to his question; more often the student will find the abbreviation וצריך עיון–וצ״ע (it needs further study). R. Akiva Eiger's comments are noted by a circle with a line drawn through it.

1.10 Additional Commentaries

Depending upon the publisher and the edition, the student may well find other commentaries on the page of the Talmud. These include:

1.10.1 ***Rabbenu Gershom*** Written by R. Gershom (France—end of 10th to beginning of 11th century). The commentary is similar in style to that of Rabbenu Chananel.

According to tradition, Rabbenu Gershom died in the year that Rashi was born. He can be seen as the spiritual founder of the French-German community. Rashi, who was a student of his disciples, R. Yaakov ben Yakar and R. Yitzchok ben Yehudah, refers to him as *Meor ha-Golah*—the light of the exile. He is best known to us by virtue of the *takkanos*—communal ordinances—attributed to him, e.g., the prohibition of bigamy, of divorcing a wife against her will, and of reading another person's mail.

1.10.2 ***Tosafos Yeshanim*** Alternative versions of the commentaries of the Tosafos.

1.10.3 ***Tosafos Rid*** Commentary written by R. Yeshaya di-Trani (Italy—13th century). R. Yeshaya's commentary was published in the margin of tractates *Kesubos* and *Gittin*. His commentary to other tractates was published separately. His halachic decisions are often quoted in the *Or Zarua* (R. Yitzchok ben Moshe of Vienna) and in the *Shibbolei ha-Leket* (by R. Tzidkiyahu ha-Rofe of Italy), which would seem to indicate that he was in close contact with both the Ashkenazic and Sephardic scholars of his day.

1.10.4 ***Tosafos Rosh*** Commentary of R. Asher ben Yechiel (see 2.2).

1.10.5 ***Shitah M'kubetzes*** Commentary of R. Betzalel Ashkenazi (see 3.7).

2

Commentaries Appended to the Talmud

While thousands of commentaries have been written on the Talmud *Bavli,* there are a number of major ones that—depending upon the publisher—have been bound together with the Talmud. Some of the commentaries are explanatory while others are more concerned with devolving the *halachah* from the discussion. It is beyond the scope of this work to examine each and every one, but it is worthwhile for the reader to become acquainted with some of the major ones.

2.1 *Piskei Tosafos*

A compendium of the halachic decisions that can be found in the commentary of Tosafos, attributed to R. Asher ben Yechiel (the Rosh).

2.2 *Rosh*

The halachic commentary of Rabbenu Asher ben Yechiel (b. Germany—1250, d. Spain—1327). A disciple of R. Meir of Ruttenberg, the Rosh fled Germany after the arrest of his teacher, settling first in

Italy and then moving on to Spain where he was in close contact with R. Shlomo ben Aderes, the Rashba.

In his halachic commentary to the Talmud, the Rosh—like the Rif before him—deals only with those parts of the Talmud that have halachic application today. He does not comment on the aggadic material included within the Talmud's discussion. As a disciple of R. Meir of Ruttenberg—one of the authors of the Tosafos—the commentary of the *Rosh* is similar to that of the Tosafos in that he too subjects the *halachah* under consideration to comparison with other talmudic sources in an attempt to discern whether there are any contradictions, which he then attempts to resolve.

Unlike the Tosafos or the Rif, the Rosh often establishes the practical *halachah* in each case, basing his decision on the principles of decision established by the Talmud itself or by citing the decisions of earlier halachic sources.

2.2.1 ***Tiferes Shmuel*** Glosses to the commentary of the Rosh by R. Aharon Shmuel Kaidanover (Maharshak) (Poland—1624–1676). Forced to flee Poland during the Chmielnicki uprising, he served together with R. Shabbesai ben Meir (the *Shach*—see 11.5) and R. Efraim Katz (author of *Sha'ar Efraim*) on the *beis din* of Vilna. Later, he moved to Germany, serving as rabbi in Fuerth and Frankfurt, before returning to Poland as *av beis din* of Cracow.

2.2.2 ***Pilpula Charifta*** Glosses to the commentary of the Rosh on *Nezikin* by R. YomTov Lipman Heller (Prague—1579–1654), author of the commentary *Tosafos Yom Tov* to the Mishnah—see 4.3. The author's commentary to the Rosh on other tractates is called *Ma'adanei Yom Tov* and *Lechem Chamudos*.

2.2.3 ***Korban Nesanel*** Glosses to the commentary of the Rosh on *Nashim* and *Mo'ed* by R. Nesanel Weil (Germany—1687–1769), rabbi and *av beis din* of Karlsruhe, Germany.

2.2.4 *ha-Gaos ha-Bach* and *ha-Gaos ha-Gra* Glosses and textual emendations by R. Yoel Sirkes (see 10.2) and R. Eliyahu, the *Gaon* of Vilna (see 11.14).

2.3 Rambam's Commentary to the Mishnah

An explanation of the major points of each *mishnah* by R. Moshe ben Maimon (see chap. 9). Originally written in Arabic as an aid to understanding the Mishnah, the Rambam began this work while still in Spain and completed it in Egypt. It was translated into Hebrew by R. Yehuda Alcharizi and others. In most cases where there is a dispute among *tanna'im* within a *mishnah,* the Rambam establishes the *halachah* according to the rules of decision that he used in his larger, purely halachic work—*Yad ha-Chazakah.*

Within the framework of the commentary to the Mishnah, the Rambam wrote a number of lengthy and comprehensive introductions that have become classics in their own right. The introduction to *Seder Zera'im* provides us with an historical overview of the *masorah* from the time of Moshe to the time of the Rambam. The introduction to *Avos* (known as *Shemoneh Perakim*) and the introduction to the eleventh *perek* of *Sanhedrin* (in which the Rambam delineates the 13 Principles of Faith) are major philosophical works.

2.4 *Maharsha*

Commentary by R. Shmuel Eidels (Poland—1555–1631), rabbi of Chelm, Lublin, and Ostrow. In his commentary, the Maharsha elaborates on the Talmud's discussion—posing questions and offering terse comments to help the student understand the question under discussion. He also elaborates on the commentaries of both Rashi and Tosafos, often offering suggestions for textual emendations so as to resolve difficulties.

The Maharsha, unlike many other talmudic commentators, also included a commentary to the aggadic portion of the Talmud in which he explains the terminology, symbolism, and meaning of the sometimes obscure aggadic passages. This commentary is usually appended to the *Ein Yaakov* as well (see 3.6). In our editions of the Talmud, the Maharsha's commentary to the *aggadah* is set in smaller type to distinguish it from his commentary to the halachic portion of the Talmud's discussion.

2.5 *Chochmas Shlomo*

Commentary by R. Shlomo Luria (Maharshal [see 12.9] Poland—1510–1574). Although it appears together with the Maharsha, the *Chochmas Shlomo* is a separate commentary, offering suggestions for textual emendations—many of which have been included in our editions of the Talmud—as well as explanations of obscure terminology. R. Yehoshua Falk (the *S'ma*—see 11.2) was his student.

2.6 *Maharam*

Glosses to the commentaries of Rashi and Tosafos by R. Meir of Lublin (Poland—1558–1616). This commentary is also usually printed alongside that of the Maharsha although it is completely separate in terms of content.

2.7 *Maharam Schiff*

Commentary to the halachic portions of the Talmud by R. Meir ben Yaakov Schiff (Germany—1605–1641), similar in style and content to the commentary of the Maharsha.

2.8 *Rashash*

Commentary by R. Shmuel ben Yosef Strashun (Lithuania—1794–

1872). A student of R. Avrahom Danzig (author of *Chayei Adam* and *Chochmas Adam*—see 13.2), the Rashash follows the style of the *Gaon* of Vilna, offering brief comments and suggestions for textual emendations to solve questions and apparent contradictions.

2.9 *Rif*

See chapter 8.

2.10 *Mordechai*

Commentary by R. Mordechai ben Hillel (Germany—1220–1298). A student of R. Meir of Ruttenberg, the Mordechai elaborated on the talmudic discussion in the style of the Tosafos, but arranged his commentary according to the *halachos* brought in the Rif (see chap. 8). He quotes extensively from the writings of his teacher, as well as from the commentaries of many others of the Tosafos, including R. Yitzchok ben Moshe (the *Or Zarua*) and Rabbenu Peretz. The published versions of the *Mordechai* usually include the annotations of R. Moshe Isserles (see Rama—11.1).

R. Mordechai was a brother-in-law of R. Meir ha-Kohen of Ruttenberg (author of *Hagaos Maimonis*—see 9.2). R. Mordechai, along with his wife and five children, was martyred *al kiddush ha-Shem* during the Rindfleisch massacre in 1298.

2.11 *Yefeh Einayim*

Compiled by R. Aryeh Leib Yellin (Poland—1820–1886) who served as rabbi of Bielsk. The work provides parallel sources in midrashic literature for the aggadic material in the Talmud as well as suggestions for textual emendations.

3

Selected Major Commentaries to the Talmud

3.1 *Ramban*

Commentary by R. Moshe ben Nachman (b. Spain—1194, d. Eretz Yisrael—1270), a disciple of R. Yitzchok ben Avraham of Dampierre (the Ri), one of the primary authors of the Tosafos. Among his students were R. Shlomo ben Aderes (the Rashba) and R. Aaron ben Yosef ha-Levi (author of *Bedek ha-Bayis* on the Rashba's *Toras ha-Bayis*—sometimes identified as the author of *Sefer ha-Chinuch*). A cousin of Rabbenu Yonah of Gerona, the Ramban defended the Rambam in the controversy surrounding the *Moreh Nevuchim* (see 16.4) led by Rabbenu Yonah and R. Shlomo Min ha-Har.

The Ramban quotes extensively from both the masters of the Spanish schools of talmudic commentators—Rabbenu Chananel, the Rif, and the Ri mi-Gash—as well as from the commentaries of the authors of the Tosafos. His commentary was a synthesis of both schools, comparing the talmudic discussion to other texts as well as seeking to derive the principles that underlie the *halachah*. At times, the Ramban goes to great length to explain the underlying principles of a specific halachic concept, e.g., his essay on *gramma* (causation) in his commentary to *Bava Basra*.

The Ramban wrote on a wide variety of subjects (see 8.5). He wrote glosses to the Rambam's *Sefer ha-Mitzvos* in which he often disagrees with the Rambam's calculation of the 613 precepts. One of his most famous works is his record of the debate (*Sefer ha-Vikuach*) with Pablo Christiani—an apostate Jew—in which he was forced to participate by order of King James of Aragon. Although promised royal protection, the Ramban's success forced him to flee Spain. He settled in Eretz Yisrael and is credited with the reestablishment of the Jewish community in Jerusalem.

3.2 *Rashba*

Commentary by R. Shlomo ben Aderes (Spain—1235–1310). A disciple of Rabbenu Yonah and the Ramban, he was the teacher of R. Yom Tov ben Avraham of Seville (the Ritva—see next entry) and R. Bachya ben Asher (author of the commentary on the Bible; not to be confused with R. Bachya ibn Paquda, author of *Chovos ha-Levavos*). The Rashba served as rabbi of Barcelona for over forty years. As religious leader of this most important community, halachic questions were addressed to him from all over Europe, and thousands of his responsa are extant (including some erroneously ascribed to the Ramban).

3.3 *Ritva*

Commentary by R. Yom Tov ben Avraham of Seville (Spain—1250–1330). A disciple of the Rashba, he served as rabbi of Saragossa and after the death of his teacher was considered the foremost talmudist in Spain.

3.4 *Beis ha-Bechirah*

A summary of the halachic materials in the Talmud, including a compendium of the commentaries of the *rishonim,* collected and edited by R. Menachem ben Shlomo Meiri (Southern France—1249–1306). R. Menachem maintained close contact with the Rashba and with Rabbenu Yonah, whom he refers to often as "my teacher."

In his *Beis ha-Bechirah* (also referred to as the *Meiri*), R. Menachem does not refer to the *rishonim* by name, but rather by epithets that he assigned. Thus, he refers to the Rif as "the greatest of *poskim,*" to Rashi as "the greatest of rabbis," to the Rambam as "the greatest of authors," and to the Ra'avad as "the greatest of commentators." He also frequently mentions "the early scholars of Narbonne" and "the early scholars of Catalonia," but it is not clear to whom he is referring. In the introduction to his commentary to tractate *Avos,* the Meiri presents the chain of Torah transmission until his time.

3.5 *Ran*

Commentary by R. Nissim ben Reuven of Gerona (Spain—1310–1375). Among his disciples was R. Chasdai Crescas (author of *Or Hashem* and teacher of R. Yosef Albo—author of *Sefer ha-Ikarim*). His commentary to *Nedarim* is his best-known work and is printed in most editions of the Talmud in place of the Tosafos. As we have already noted, the commentary of Rashi to *Nedarim* is considered to be erroneous; the Ran's commentary is used in its stead. He also wrote a commentry to the Rif (see 8.7).

3.6 *Ein Yaakov*

Compilation of the aggadic material appearing in the Talmud by

R. Yaakov Ibn Chaviv (1445–1515). R. Yaakov was born in Spain, but fled in the expulsion in 1492, settling in Salonika where he headed a yeshivah as well as serving as rabbi of the Spanish community. When he began his compilation of the *aggadah,* he withdrew from all communal activity. The published *Ein Yaakov* includes his commentary—*Iyun Yaakov*—which is based on the works of the *rishonim*. Most of the *Ein Yaakov* was published by the author's son, R. Levi Ibn Chaviv (Ralbach), who served as rabbi in Jerusalem and led the opposition to the reintroduction of *semichah* by R. Yaakov Beirav of Tzefas.

3.7 *Shitah M'kubetzes*

A compendium of the commentaries of the *rishonim,* collected and edited by R. Betzalel Ashkenazi (1520–1591). Born in Eretz Yisrael, R. Betzalel moved to Cairo, where he studied under R. Dovid ibn Zimra (Radvaz—see 9.5). He was a colleague of the poet, R. Yisroel Najara—author of *Yah Ribbon Olam*. R. Betzalel founded a yeshivah in Cairo among whose students was R. Yitzchok Luria—the *Ari ha-Kadosh*. In 1587 he returned to Eretz Yisrael and succeeded R. Chaim Vital as head of the rabbinical court of Jerusalem.

In his *Shitah M'kubetzes* (literally, collected opinions), R. Betzalel quotes extensively from the commentaries of Rabbenu Gershom, Rabbenu Chananel, and R. Yosef Ibn mi-Gash and is often our only source for these commentaries.

3.8 *Chidushei Aggados* of the Maharal

Commentary to the *aggados* of the Babylonian Talmud by R. Yehudah Loew ben Betzalel (b. Posen—1525, d. Prague—1609). Among his many disciples was R. Yom Tov Lipman Heller (author of *Tosafos Yom Tov* to the Mishnah).

While *Chidushei Aggados* was written specifically as a commentary to the *aggadah*—explaining the symbolism and meaning of the texts—almost all of the Maharal's works can be seen as being expositions on the *aggadah*. These include *Nesivos Olam, Derech Chaim* on *Avos, Tiferes Yisrael, Be'er ha-Golah, Netzach Yisrael, Gevuros ha-Shem, Or Chadash,* and *Ner Mitzvah*. The Maharal also wrote a supercommentary to Rashi's commentary to *Chumash* (*Gur Aryeh*).

3.9 *Pnei Yehoshua*

Commentary by R. Yaakov Yehoshua Falk (b. Poland—1680, d. Germany—1756). In the introduction to the *Pnei Yehoshua,* the author recounts that after his wife and daughter were killed in an explosion, he decided to dedicate his life to Torah study. In 1717 he became rabbi of Lemberg, succeeding R. Tzvi Hirsh Ashkenazi (*Chacham Tzvi*), and established a yeshivah. A vociferous opponent of the Shabbateans, R. Yaakov Yehoshua was forced to leave Lemberg, serving a number of communities until he settled in Frankfurt where he became involved in the dispute between R. Yaakov Emden and R. Yonasan Eybeschutz.

In his masterwork *Pnei Yehoshua,* R. Yaakov Yehoshua explains many of the difficult discussions in the Talmud as well as providing a commentary to both Rashi and Tosafos. In his introduction, he stresses that he wrote his commentary to provide students with a tool to understand the works of the *rishonim* and to answer those questions that Tosafos had left unresolved.

3.10 *R. Akiva Eiger*

Commentary by R. Akiva Eiger (Bohemia—1761–1837). In 1814, he became rabbi of Posen—serving as unofficial chief rabbi of the entire district. He established a yeshivah that became the leading center for study in Central Europe. R. Moshe Sofer (*Chasam Sofer*) was his son-in-law.

R. Akiva Eiger was a prolific author. *Gilyon ha-Shas* (see 1.9) and his notes to the Mishnah were published in his lifetime. His more extensive commentary to the Talmud (*Drush ve-Chidush*), his responsa, and his glosses to the *Shulchan Aruch* were published by his children.

4

The Mishnah and Its Commentaries

While the Mishnah is most often studied in conjunction with the *gemara*—especially once the student has been introduced to the latter—there are many tractates in the Babylonian Talmud for which we do not have a *gemara* text, e.g., most of the orders of *Zera'im* and *Taharos*. As already noted, the earliest complete manuscript of the Talmud extant dates from the fourteenth century. Our editions of the Talmud match that manuscript except for minor textual emendations and changes imposed by the censors. We have no earlier fragments of *gemara* from other tractates nor are there any references to missing tractates in commentaries that predate the Munich manuscript. Thus, it is not unreasonable to assume that our *gemara* is complete.

Our study of some tractates then, at least within the framework of the Babylonian Talmud, is limited to the text of the Mishnah. On page 31 is a sample reproduced from the Romm Vilna edition of the Mishnah. In terms of the division into separate *mishnayos,* the text in this edition differs at times from the text of the Mishnah quoted in editions that include the *gemara.* Usually, the *mishnayos* cited within the text of the *gemara* are shorter than those cited in volumes of the Mishnah alone.

The *mishnayos* themselves are the subject of many commentaries written specifically as study aids independent of the *gemara*. As we have already seen (see 2.3), the Rambam wrote a major commentary on the Mishnah alone. Other commentaries with which the student should be familiar include:

4.1 *Rash*

Commentary to the *mishnayos* of *Zera'im* and *Taharos* by R. Shimshon of Sens (b. France—1150, d. Acco—1215). A disciple of the Ri, R. Shimshon is one of the major contributors to the Tosafos on the Talmud and is quoted as the Rashba (not to be confused with R. Shlomo ben Aderes—see 3.2). As a result of the persecutions during the Crusades, R. Shimshon moved with a group of his colleagues to Eretz Yisrael in 1211. His commentary is usually printed opposite that of the Rambam in the Vilna edition of the Talmud.

4.2 *Bartinura*

Commentary by R. Ovadiah of Bertinoro (b. Italy—1445, d. Jerusalem—1510). While we know almost nothing of his background, we do know that he left his home in 1485 to travel to Eretz Yisrael, which he only reached in 1488. During his travels, he wrote a number of letters (published under the title *Darkei Tzion*) to his family, describing the various Jewish communities that he visited in Sicily, Greece, and Egypt.

R. Ovadiah wrote his commentary to the Mishnah (popularly referred to as the *Rav*) in Jerusalem where he served as spiritual head of the community. In it, he quotes extensively from Rashi's commentary to the Talmud as well as from the Rambam. The commentary is simi-

בה יד). **אם משנתנה לו אמר אני זכיתי בה תחלה** טו). **לא אמר כלום** טז): ד **ראה את המציאה. ונפל עליה. ובא אחר והחזיק בה. זה שהחזיק בה זכה בה** יז). **ראה אותן רצין אחר מציאה** יח). **אחר צבי שבור. אחר גוזלות** יט) **שלא פרחו** כ). **ואמר זכתה לי שדי. זכתה לו** כא). **היה צבי רץ**

הרוכב. ואין המגביה יכול לומר אני זכיתי בה: **לא אמר כלום.** שקנאה זה שמשכה מיד חברו. וכל זמן שהיתה ביד המגביה הפקר היתה: ד **זה שהחזיק בה זכה בה.** ודוקא שהיתה המציאה ברשות הרבים. שאין ארבע אמות של אדם קונות לו ברה"ר. לפיכך המחזיק בה זכה. אבל בסימטא שהיא בצד של יחיד או בצדי רשות הרבים באין רבים דוחקים שם ארבע אמות של אדם קונות לו כל מציאה וכל הפקר שבתוך לו בארבע אמות ואין אחר רשאי לתפסו. ותקינו ליה רבנן כי היכי דלא ליתו לאנצויי: **אחר צבי שבור.** שאינו יכול לרוץ ומשהו בתוך השדה אם לא יטלוהו אחרים והוי כמציאה: **זכתה לו.** שדהו. והוא שעומד בצד שדהו וגנון שיכול לרוץ אחריו

תליא בכונת הגבהתו לצורך מי היתה. כך נראה בעיני. [*ולפי נאמר שר' יוחנן יחלוק על סברא זו אלא שמתרץ המשנה בתירוץ מרווח יותר. דתירוץ דלעיל דחוק והא לא תנן תחלה וכדדחי לי' בסוגיא מה"ש. ושוב מצאתי בתשובה להרשב"א שהביאה הב"י סימן קל"ה שכתב אדרבי יוחנן דטעמו דמלי שמגביה לומר כשאמרת תנה לי לא היה בדעתי שאמרת שתזכה בה בשבילך אלא נאחר שהגבהתה ותתננה לך. עכ"ל. ובלומר ומשום כך לא נתכוונתי לזכות לך בהגבהתי. כך נ"ל]: **אם משנתנה** לו אמר אני זכיתי בה תחלה. מפרש בגמרא דמשום רישא דמיירי דוקא באמר תחלה כדכתבתי לעיל הלכך דייק בסיפא למתני תחלה כלומר ואם משנתנה לו טוען אותה טענה דרישא. אבל משום סיפא לא איצטריך למיתני פשטא תחלה דאפילו אי לא טען תחלה משמעתא תחלה קאמר. דמי מ"י למימר אני זכה בה פעשו ואלא איט בידו. [תי"ט]. [*ולפי מה שכתבתי לעיל לדרבי יוחנן אין צריך לזה התירוץ דאמר תחלה אדרבא רישא אין הכי נמי דלא אמר תחלה ואפ"ה מצי הדר ביה כיון שאמר תנה לי ולא אמר זכה לי. וקתני בסיפא תחלה. לגלויי דרישא אף בלא אמר תחלה]: ד **זה שהחזיק בה זכה בה.** כתב הר"ב ודוקא שהיתה המציאה ברשות הרבים וכו' כלן חזר בו מפירוש הבני שכתב במ"ג פ"ד דפאה דטעמא משום דנפל עליה וכו'. ע"ש. וטעמא שאין ד' אמות קונות ברשות הרבים. כתב רש"י שהרי אין לאדם שם ארבע אמות מיוחדות שהרבים עוברים יש לו בתוכה עומדים אצלו. ע"כ. ומ"ש הר"ב אבל בסימטא שהוא שביל היחיד. או בצדי רה"ר וכו'. ובמשנה ד' פ"ק דקדושין כתב בסמטא שהיא זוית של רשות הרבים וכן פירש"י שם [דף כ"ה ע"ב]. ולפי זה לצדי רשות הרבים הוא הסמוך לכותים אע"פ שאינו בזוית. אלא בזוית שפני איניש אהדדי מכ' הרחובות ולפיכך נמשכים אגל הזוית שלא לדחוק זה את זה. וזה מגרי יותר מבצדי רה"ר. ומן שני לצדי הרחוב. לפיכך נתיחד שם לזוית בפני עצמה. אבל לפירש הר"ב דהכא גם הזווית בכלל לצדי רשות הרבים יחשב. והרמב"ם בפ"ס דבבא בתרא דף פ"ד כתב היא דאמר שביל של יחיד. ואני שמעתי כניסה טולמת מרבות הרבים. ויש רשות לבני אדם להעמיד שם חפצים כלהם כחצר השותפין דאיפ עשוי להלוך בני רה"ר. ע"כ. ויתכן לומר דזהו דנקטי רש"י והר"ב דהיינו בלימט. וא"ד שביל וכו' דברי הערוך הן. וכתב שהוא לשון לעז ממש. ע"כ. ונ"ל דשביל של יחיד שאמרו אין הכוונה שהוא של יחיד. דאין סברא לומר דתקנו ד' אמות בשדה דבעל הבית לא תקנו ליה רבנן והעתיקה הר"ב בפ"ד דפאה [משנה ג'] ומשום דין פאה נקט דבעל הבית. אבל לענין מציאה כל אדם יש לו בעל לא תקנו. וכמ"ש הרמב"ם בפי"ז מהלכות גזלה. וכתב ל"י בגמרא אלא שביל של רבים ובוונא דהניק ברפ"ב דפאה. שביל היחיד ושביל הרבים: **אחר צבי שבור.** פירושא דרישא. וז"ל הרמב"ם בפי"ז מהלכות אבידה מי שראה אחרים רצים אחר המציאה והרי היא לגבי שבור וכו': **ואמר** זכתה לי שדי. ואע"ג דבארבע אמות דתקנו רבנן דקונות לו אע"ג דלא אמר כלום כתב המגיד שם [הלכה י"א] משום דחלישא קנייה דבארבע אמות עפי מפני שהוא יכול לנטות עלמו וליטלה. ע"כ. ועיין מ"ש במשנה ג' פ"ב. והב"י סימן רס"ח כתב טעם אחר דארבע אמות שאני דכיון דמשום דלא אתי לאנצויי תקנו רבנן דליקני. לא ראו לחלק בין אמר ללא אמר. דא"כ אכתי אתי לאנצויי. ע"כ. אבל התוספות והרא"ש סברי דמתניתין לאו דוקא וה"ה כי לא אמר נמי קני. והא דקתני ואמר זכתה לי בשביל למעט הרצים אחריה אמר כן: **זכתה לו.** מסקינן בגמרא דחצר משום שליחות הוא והא דברים פ"ח דגטין פירש הר"ב משום דבעינן למיקני. *משום קטן וקטנה איצטריך קרא לרבינהו בתורת יד משום דליתנהו בתורת שליחות ומשום הכי נמי בעינן שתהא עומדת בצדה אפילו בחצר המשתמרת כמ"ש הר"ב שם משום דבעינן דומיא דידה. אבל מ"ש הר"ב בכאן והוא שעומד בצד שדהו. גמרא. היינו פירושא דמשתמר בתוך שדהו שכתב בדעת הקודם דלא בעינן הכא תרתי. שיהא משתמר. ושיעמוד בצד שדהו. והיינו טעמא דמצריך נמי שיכול לרוץ אחריה ומגיען וכו' דלאי לאו הכי כי עומד בצד שדהו מאי הוי. שמע מינה דטעמא דבעינן עומד וכו' משום דהיאי משתמרת. וכתב ל"י דמשתמרת ואינו עומד בצדה דלא הוי ידו אלא מתורת שליחות בלבד [צריכא טעמא] למה תזכה לו במציאתו דלמי נעשה שליח. לבעל הממון אינו שליח. שהרי אין כאן בעל הממון. ולא שייך נמי למימר בחצר. כדאמר גבי מגביה מציאה לחבירו. דמגו דזכי לנפשיה. זכי נמי לחבריה. *וכתב הרנב"ר ז"ל דאיכא למימר דכל שהיא משתמרת למי שהוא זכות לו כידו היא

יכין **תפארת ישראל** יכין

יד) ודוקא באמר תנה לי, שלא רצה לזכות בה עד שתבוא לידו, ולהכי אף שמתכוין שמגביה להרוכב, יכול לחזור בו קודם שיתנה לו, אבל באמר זכה לי מדהגביה זה בשתיקה, נתכוין שיהיה להרוכב, ואינו יכול לחזור בו. מיהו באמר בשעת הגבהה או קודם לכן לעצמי אגביה, קנה [רמ"ש], וי"א דה"ה בידע שהורה בזול ואמר לחבירו קנה אותה לנו וקנה סתם קנו שניהן, וי"א דבאין מעוה לרמאין לא קנה. דלא דמי למציאה שיכול לטלה בעצמו [שם]: טו) ר"ל קודם שהגבהתיה נתכוונתי לזכותה לעצמי: טז) נ"ל דמה"ש לא קאמר הינו נאמן דקמ"ל דאפילו נאמינא שכך חשב, ולא הגביהה לצורך חבירו, עכ"פ גם הוא עצמו לא קנאה, מדלא אמר תחלה בפירוש לעצמי אגביהה, וס"ל כהפקר עד שנתנה להרוכב, וקנאה הרוכב במשיכה, והייט דקמ"ל רק כולה מתניתין [עי' גיטין פ"א מ"ו]: יז) ודוקא ברה"ר או בשדה חבירו, אבל בצידי ר"ה, או בסימטא [והוא זוית שבולטת בר"ה], שד' אמות קונות שם, קנה. וי"א מדנפל עליה לא קנה ליה ד' אמות בשום מקום [רמ"ח]: יח) דהיינו אחר וכו': יט) נקט לשון רבים מדרכן לפרוח ולילך הרבה ביחד ועוד משום שכן הרבה יש רבים הרלין לזכות בהן: כ) שבו אגו כשלא יטלים אחרים, ישתמרו בשדהו: כא) וקיי"ל דחצר המשתמרת

ד ראה את המציאה. ה"א פ"י פ"ז פ' גזילה ואבידה ל"א פפ"ג סמ"ג עשין כ"ד ט"ו: ח"מ פי' רס"ח סעי' א': ראה אותן רצים. י"א כ"א פ"י פ"ז הל' אבידה הל' י"א ספ"ג עשין כ"ד טוש"ע ח"מ סי' רס"ח סעי' ד':

שנויי נוסחאות

אם משנתנה. בכי"ק ובכי"מ ואם. **אמר אני זכיתי.** בכי"ק אומר.. (בה) תחלה. בד"נ ליתא. ד **ונפל.** בד"נ ובכי"מ ובמשנ"י ונפל לו. **זה שהחזיק.** בכי"מ מי שהחזיק. **אחר מציאה.** בד"נ ובכי"מ ופ' ובכת"פ.. המציאה. **אחר גוזלות.** בכי"ק ובכי"ר ואחר.. **שלא פרחו.** בכי"ק שלא הפריחו. **זכתה.** בד"נ ובכי"ק ובכת"פ זכת בכל המשנ'. **זכתה לו.** בכי"פ זכתה לו שדהו.

תוספות חדשים

ד בתוי"ט ד"ה ואמר זכתה לי כו' והא דקתני ט'. כן כתב הרא"ש *) אבל התוס' כתבו דנקט אמר משום רישא דאפי' אמר כיון דהן כורס לא קני:

תוספות רע"ק

לא הוי כזכה לי. אבל בלא אמר לו כלל והוא הגביה לחבירו ולא אמר כן בשעת הגבהה או מקודם גם מעיקרא ס"ל דל"ק ופשוט. אח"כ ראיתי שגם הש"ך שם כ"כ: ד [אות ח] תוי"ט ד"ה זכתה לו. משום קטן וקטנה. בלא"ה אף בגדולה איצטריך דהא אשה יוצאה שלא לרצונה וע"י שליחות א"י לגרשה בע"כ דאין חבין לאדם אלא בפניו ואיצטריך קרא לרבות חצר בעושרת בצדו משום ידה. ואם זרק לה הגט בחצר כוה בע"כ דידה מגורשת: [אות ט] בא"ד וכתב הרנב"ר ז"ל דאיכא למימר. קשה לי הא מבואר בסתי' דלא ילפינן קטן מקטנה והיינו דרק באשה אתרבאי חצר משום יד אבל לא באיש. חבי קיי"ל בש"ע סי' רס"ח וא"כ

*) וז"ל התוי"ט בפלפולא חריפתא על דברי הרא"ש שאמר דבשביל למעט הרלים וכו'. ואפי' ההוא תהני' למאי צריכא ולכך נראה כדברי התוס' דמשום רישא איצטריך דבסיפא אפשוטין דאפילו הכי לא קנה עכ"ל.

lar in concept to that of Rashi, being primarily concerned with explaining the text of the Mishnah.

4.3 *Tosafos Yom Tov*

Commentary by R. Yom Tov Lipman Heller (b. Bavaria—1579, d. Cracow—1654). A disciple of the Maharal of Prague, his commentary serves to expand that of the *Rav* by analyzing the text and offering the opinions of *rishonim* whom the *Rav* does not quote. It also serves as a *tosafos,* comparing the text of the Mishnah to other sources and explaining apparent contradictions.

R. Yom Tov also wrote *Megillas Aivah*—a vivid, biographical account of his experiences as rabbi in Prague, Nikolsburg, Nemerov, and Cracow and of the tumultuous events that occurred in the wake of the Chmielnicki massacres. He served on the permanent *beis din* of the Council of the Four Lands and was responsible for many of the *takkanos* introduced by that body.

4.4 *Meleches Shlomo*

Commentary by R. Shlomo Adani (b. Yemen—1567, d. Tzefas—1625), a disciple of R. Chaim Vital and R. Betzalel Ashkenazi.

4.5 *Tiferes Yisroel*

Commentary by R. Yisroel Lifschitz (Germany—1782–1860). R. Yisroel served as rabbi in a number of German communities; his last position was in Danzig. He divided his commentary into two sections. In one he explains terms and phrases and often quotes the commentary of the *Rav* verbatim. The second part offers a longer and more detailed explanation of the Mishnah. These two sections were called *Yachin* and

Boaz—after the two pillars that supported the *Beis ha-Mikdash*—and the Vilna edition of the Mishnah is often referred to by that name.

R. Yisroel also wrote a number of introductions to various themes in the Mishnah that are particularly useful for the student; e.g., *Kalkeles Shabbos,* in which he outlines the concepts of work forbidden on *Shabbos,* and *Derush Or ha-Chaim* (which is printed after tractate *Sanhedrin*), in which he deals with the concepts of resurrection and the compatibility of tradition and scientific discovery. (An English translation of the latter was recently published by the Association of Orthodox Jewish Scientists.)

4.6 *Tosafos R. Akiva Eiger*

Textual emendations and brief comments by R. Akiva Eiger (see 3.10).

4.7 *Tosafos Rishon Letzion*

Emendations by R. Yeshayahu Pick (Germany—1725–1799) that also provide the student with extensive cross-references. The rabbi of Breslau, Germany, R. Yeshayahu wrote extensive glosses to almost the entire body of rabbinic literature—including the Talmud (see 1:6), the Rif, the *Aruch,* and the Mishnah. As noted, some of his work is a reediting of the earlier work by R. Yehoshua Boaz.

The standard Vilna edition of the Mishnah also has a number of additional commentaries and glosses added by the publishers, which include:

4.8 *Tziunim*

References to enable the student to find the relevant citations in halachic literature.

4.9 *Tosafos Anshei Shem*

A compendium of commentaries to the Mishnah drawn from the *rishonim*.

4.10 *Shinuei Nuschaos*

Alternative texts drawn from various manuscripts of the Mishnah.

5

The Talmud *Yerushalmi* and Its Commentaries

The Talmud *Yerushalmi* consists of the discussions of the Mishnah by the *amora'im* of the academies of Eretz Yisrael. The text of the Mishnah quoted in the *Yerushalmi* often differs from the parallel text quoted in the Talmud *Bavli*—linguistically, in terms of content, and in terms of the sages quoted.

The Talmud *Yerushalmi* was closed more than a century before the Talmud *Bavli*. This was due to the political situation in Eretz Yisrael at the end of the fourth century C.E. The academies of Tzippori and Lod were destroyed, and the population of the country was subject to intense persecution by the Roman rulers of the land. This created an atmosphere that was hardly conducive to study, and though academies continued to exist in Eretz Yisrael, they were far less productive than the academies of Bavel.

The Rif (end of commentary to tractate *Eruvin*) writes:

> Because our [i.e., the *Bavli*] *gemara* is of later origin and permits it [the causing of a sound on *Shabbos*], it does not matter that the *Yerushalmi* for-

> bids it, for they [the *amora'im* of Bavel] were aware of what was said there and had they not held that it [the ruling of the academies in Eretz Yisrael] was not to be relied upon, they would not have permitted it.

This statement is the basis for our establishment of *halachah,* i.e., in cases of disagreement between the *Yerushalmi* and the *Bavli,* we follow the ruling of the latter. This would seem to have been the consensus of opinion prior to the Rif as well, for we find that Rav Hai *Gaon* (quoted in *Teshuvas ha-Gaonim* #46) writes that decisions of the *Yerushalmi* are to be ignored when they conflict with the *Bavli.*

Our texts of the *Yerushalmi* are based on the Bromberg edition (published in 1524, after the first printing of the complete *Bavli* by the same publisher), which was based on the Leyden manuscript. Interestingly, while we do not find references in the works of the *geonim* or the *rishonim* to portions of the *Bavli* that are not included in the Munich manuscript, we do find such references to texts of the *Yerushalmi* that are not included in the Leyden manuscript. Thus, Tosafos (*Niddah* 66a, s.v. *ve-tivdok*) quotes a *Yerushalmi* from the seventh chapter of that tractate, whereas the Leyden manuscript only includes the first three chapters of tractate *Niddah.* This would seem to suggest that there were once more extensive versions of the *Yerushalmi* available. The Rambam (Introduction to the commentary to the *mishnayos* of *Seder Zera'im*) writes:

> The *Bavli* is missing *gemaros* on all of *Seder Zera'im* except for tractate *Berachos*, parts of *Seder Mo'ed* (tractate *Shekalim*), *Seder Nezikin* (tractates *Eiduyos* and *Avos*), *Seder Kodshim* (tractates *Middos* and *Kinnim*) and all of *Taharos* except for tractate *Niddah,* but the *Yerushalmi* is complete for the first five *Sedarim.*

It is clear that the Rambam had a more complete version than has come down to our times, for we have no manuscripts of the *Yerushalmi*

נר 6 מראה הפנים **שנים אוחזין פרק ראשון בבא מציעא** פני משה מערבי

הלכה ד׳ ראה את המציאה ונפל לו עליה ובא אחר והחזיק בה זה שהחזיק בה זכה בה ראה אותן רצין אחר המציאה אחר צבי שבור אחר גוזלות שלא פירחו ואמר זכת לי שדי זכת לו היה צבי רץ כדרכו או שהיו הגוזלות מפריחין ואמר זכת לי שדי לא אמר כלום :

גמ׳ ר״ש לקיש אמר אבא כהן ברדליה אדם זכה במציאה בתוך ד׳ אמות שלו רבי יוחנן אמר והוא שתפול לתוך ידו מתניתא פליגא ע׳ ריש לקיש נפל מקצת הפיאה וחרק בשאר אין לו בה כלום אמר תיפתר בשלא אמר יזכו לי בד׳ אמות שלי ומור דבתרה נפל עליה ופרס טליתו עלי׳ מעבירין אותו ממנה עוד היא בשלא אמר יזכו לי בד׳ אמות שלי והתני רבי חייה שנים שהיו מתבתשין בעומר ובא עני וחטפו מלפניהן זכה בו עוד היא בשלא אמ׳ יזכו לי בד׳ אמות שלי והתנינן ראה את המציאה ונפל עליה ובא אחר והחזיק בה זה שהחזיק בה זכה בה עוד היא בשלא אמר יזכו לי בד׳ אמות שלי והתנינן קרוב לה מגורשת קרוב לו אינה מגורש׳ מחצה למחצ׳ מגורש׳ ואינה מגורשת חזקיה אמר בשכר הליבלר היא מתניתא התיכן והכתיב ואני בעניי הכינותי וגו׳ והיכי אם בנתתין בתוך ידו עשיר הוא אי בשאינן נתונין לתוך ידו יש אדם מקדיש דבר שאינו שלו הוי אומר בנתונין בתוך ד׳ אמות שלו אמר רבי אבין מהו בעניי שאין עשירות לפני מי שאמר והיה העולם דבר אחר שהיה מתענה ומקדיש סעודתו לשמים תני האומר יזכה לי ביתי במציא׳ שנפלה לתוכה לא אמר כלום יצא שם למציאתו דבריו קיימין כהדא אריסיה דרבי בא בר מינא סליק לדיקלא אשכח גוזלין ונסתון אזל שאיל לרב לא א״ל כלום אזל חזר אמר רבי בא בר מינא קשייא לן הדיתא חזר ותייתר ממציאתו :

הלכה ה׳ מציאת בנו ובתו הקטנים ועבדו ושפחתו הכנענים ומציאת אשתו הרי אילו שלו מציאת בנו ובתו הגדולים ועבדו ושפחתו העברים מציאת אשתו שגירשה אף על פי שלא נתן לה כתובתה הרי אילו שלהן :

גמ׳ א״ר יוחנן בשאינן סמוכין לאביהן אבל אם היו סמוכין לאביהן מציאתן שלו ריש לקיש אמר אין אדם זוכה לחבירו במציאה א״ר לא דמר ר״ש אבן אלא דקשי ליה על הדא דתני רבי

Yerushalmi

to *Seder Kodshim*. The version published in 1905 was proven to be a brilliant forgery.

The sample of the text on the preceding page is representative of what has become the traditional presentation of the Talmud *Yerushalmi*. The folio chosen (*Bava Metzia* 5) is a reproduction from the Slavuta edition, as printed in Zhitomir in 1865. The reader will notice a number of significant differences between the *Yerushalmi* and the parallel presentation in the *Bavli*.

The *Bavli* introduces the Mishnah with the notation מתני'; the *Yerushalmi* refers to the Mishnah as הלכה—*halachah*. The text of the Mishnah cited in the *Yerushalmi* often differs from the parallel text in the *Bavli*. The Talmud's discussion of the Mishnah in the *Yerushalmi* is far shorter than that in the *Bavli*. For reference purposes, sources in the *Yerushalmi* are indicated by quoting the chapter number and relevant *halachah*, rather than the folio as is the case with the *Bavli*.

Although numerous references to the *Yerushalmi* are made in almost all of the works of the *rishonim*, there are few commentaries that were written in that period on the text itself. The Slavuta edition offers the following commentaries:

5.1 *Pnei Moshe* and *Mar'eh Panim*

The major commentaries to the *Yerushalmi* by R. Moshe Margolis (Lithuania—18th century), teacher of R. Eliyahu of Vilna (the Vilna *Gaon*). R. Moshe's work was divided into sections: *Pnei Moshe*, in which he explains the text in the style of Rashi's commentary to the Talmud *Bavli*, and *Mar'eh Panim*, in which he compares the *Yerushalmi* with the parallel discussions in the *Bavli*. The latter commentary also cites the opinions and rulings of the *rishonim*.

5.2 *Korban Edah*

Explanatory commentary by R. Dovid Frankl (Germany—1707–1762) to *Mo'ed* and *Nashim*. Born in Berlin, R. Dovid became rabbi of Dessau in 1737 where Moses Mendelssohn was his pupil. In 1743, he was appointed chief rabbi of Berlin.

5.3 *Ein Mishpat, Masores ha-Shas,* and *Gilyon ha-Shas*

Compiled by R. Mordechai Zev Ettinger (Poland—1804–1863) and R. Yosef Shaul Natanson (Poland—1810–1875). The three works are the fruit of twenty-five years of collaboration between these two brothers-in-law. *Ein Mishpat* provides references to halachic literature, *Masores ha-Shas* provides cross-references to the parallel discussions in the Talmud *Bavli,* while *Gilyon ha-Shas* are glosses. This joint effort came to an end in 1859 when R. Mordechai Zev joined in R. Shlomo Kluger's ban on using machine *matzahs* on Pesach and R. Yosef Shaul issued a ruling permitting their use. After the deaths of R. Akiva Eiger and R. Moshe Sofer, R. Yosef Shaul was looked upon as the foremost halachic authority in Central Europe. His responsa (*Sho'el U'meishiv* and *Yosef Da'as*) contain his halachic correspondence with the great scholars of his generation.

5.4 *Ridvaz*

Commentary by R. Yaakov Dovid Willowski (b. Lithuania—1845, d. Tzefas—1913). R. Yaakov Dovid served as rabbi in a number of communities, including Vilna where he was the official *moreh tzedek*. The title was given to the city's spiritual leader, for Vilna—after a series of controversies that caused a rift in the community at the end of the eighteenth century—had no official chief rabbi. After establishing a yeshivah in Slutsk that was later headed by R. Isser Zalman Meltzer, he moved to the United States in 1903, settling in Chicago. Disappointed by the state of religious life in the United States, he left in 1905, settling in Tzefas where he founded a yeshivah.

6

The *Tosefta*

The *tosefta* (literally, additions) is composed of *beraisos* arranged according to the order of the Mishnah. In many cases, the *tosefta* is quoted in the *gemara*, and as we have already seen, its introduction is noted by use of the term תנא—we learned. However, the *tosefta* that the student will find appended to the back of complete editions of the Talmud contains a great deal of material that is not directly linked to the Mishnah nor quoted anywhere in the *gemara*. In addition, the complete *tosefta* contains much aggadic material, which is rarely the case in the Mishnah.

According to tradition, the *tosefta* was written or redacted by R. Oshiyah and R. Chiyah—two of the prominent disciples of R. Yehudah ha-Nasi, the final editor of the Mishnah. There is a great deal of scholarly controversy as to when the *tosefta* was finally edited, for our editions are replete with differences between the quotations from the *tosefta* cited in both the *Bavli* and the *Yerushalmi*.

Among the many commentaries, please note the following:

6.1 *Chasdei Dovid*

Commentary by R. Dovid Pardo (b. Venice—1718, d. Jerusalem—

1790). R. Dovid served as rabbi in Sarajevo before traveling to Jerusalem where he headed the Chesed l'Avraham yeshivah. His son married the daughter of R. Yosef Chaim Dovid Azulai (the Chida).

6.2 *Chazon Yechezkel*

Commentary by R. Yechezkel Abramsky (b. Lithuania—1886, d. Jerusalem—1976). A student of R. Chaim Soloveitchik of Brisk, R. Abramsky served as rabbi in Smolensk and Slutsk. Arrested as a counter-revolutionary after the Russian revolution, he was banished to Siberia. Upon his release, he moved to London where he headed the *beis din*. He later moved to Eretz Yisrael and served as *rosh yeshivah* of Slobodka.

II

HALACHIC LITERATURE

The *gemara,* as we shall see in Part IV, is often concerned with developing the subjects discussed in the Mishnah so that cases not specifically mentioned can be adjudicated based on a comparison to the law to which the Mishnah refers. In a sense, the *gemara* provides the framework through which *halachah* can be developed based on the derivation of the underlying principles that govern the case cited in the Mishnah. For example, the Mishnah (*Bava Metzia* 7:8) deals with the Torah laws pertaining to *shomerim*—watchmen or guardians of property—and establishes that there are four classes of watchmen whose obligations differ. The *gemara* further refines when each of these *shomerim* is considered to have been negligent in fulfilling his responsibilities and is therefore liable for damages caused to the property. Based on this refinement, halachic criteria can be established delineating culpability in other cases.

Although the subject of discussion in the Talmud is often *halachah,* neither the Mishnah nor the *gemara* can be seen as codes of law. The Mishnah usually describes a law by providing a specific example of its application, and the *gemara's* discussion is usually more concerned with determining the basis for the law—either logically or through scriptural exegesis—rather than in establishing a codex per se. By studying and mastering the talmudic discussion and its logical basis, however, one can develop a system of legislation that can cover every conceivable situation.

In a sense, the Talmud establishes the framework through which the subsequent legislator—which can be either a court of law or an individual person attempting to understand what he is obligated to do in a specific situation—can establish his ruling, confident that he is acting in accordance with the intent of the Torah. If the Torah might be compared to a constitution providing guidelines for acceptable behavior, the Talmud should be seen as providing an outline of the structures that all subsequent legislation must follow.

In the period during which the Talmud developed—and we use the term developed for it was a process that took generations—various schools of thought expressed their opinions. Many of the discussions recorded in the Talmud are attempts to establish which of these schools of thought are correct in the sense that their opinions are consistent with the Torah's intent. In most cases, the Talmud does not specify whether the *halachah* follows one opinion or the other. However, the Talmud does at times delineate some general criteria for establishing *halachah,* e.g., the resolution of the dispute between Abbaye and Rava in Abbaye's favor.

In the analysis of a talmudic discussion (see chap. 20), we examine the dispute between Abbaye and Rava regarding lost property. The discussion there is typical of the style of the Talmud in that both Abbaye and Rava are forced to justify their opinions in the face of earlier discussions of other sages. Neither Abbaye nor Rava could reject the earlier rulings as being incorrect. Abbaye, for example, could not say that he was unconcerned that a *mishnah,* a *beraisa,* or a *tosefta* seemed to contradict his opinion, for the essence of the halachic process is consistency. He was therefore forced to logically establish that his ruling was consistent with accepted precedent. Were he unable to do so—as was the case ultimately with Rava—the very inability to substantiate his ruling in the face of external materials was proof that his opinion was invalid.

The discussion between Abbaye and Rava does not necessarily reflect a disagreement as to how to adjudicate a specific case. We have no reason to assume that the academy had been presented, in that instance, with a question that pertained to something that had actually transpired. Rather, it would seem that having studied the Mishnah, the academy began discussing a theoretical question: Would a person be required to declare that he had found lost property and thus give the owner an opportunity to reclaim it if it could be assumed that the owner—were he aware of his loss—would give up hope of recovery?

To be sure, there are instances where we find that the Talmud records specific halachic decisions that are the result of questions that had been sent for clarification. For example, the Talmud (*Yevamos* 104b–105a) notes that Shmuel's father received an answer regarding a question. The manner in which this is recorded in the Talmud would seem to suggest that a specific question had been sent for decision, for the Talmud records there that he received a second response that further clarified the question (see Tosafos, s.v. *yevamah*). There are also numerous instances where the Talmud's discussion of a question is prefaced with the phrase שלחו מתם—they sent from there (i.e., from Bavel to Israel)—which indicates that the academies and schools dealt with specific questions sent to them for decision. However, it would seem that these questions and the subsequent discussions are recorded to provide us with a means of understanding how the *halachah* was developed rather than being cited as a code of law or practice.

Literature that is specifically halachic begins with the period following the sealing of the Talmud *Bavli*. During the period of the *geonim*, which followed the final editing of the Talmud, the yeshivos of Bavel continued to function and flourish. However, they no longer existed as a framework in which the Mishnah was discussed and elucidated. In addition to their traditional roles as educational institutions, the academies also served as legislative courts to which questions could be addressed for resolution during the study sessions.

While there was similar halachic inquiry during the period of the *amora'im,* we have no independent body of literature outside of the Talmud that records these halachic questions. Thus, while some of the aggadic material in *Midrash Rabbah,* for example, is also recorded in the Talmud, we do not find a nontalmudic collection of the questions sent to the yeshivahs in Eretz Yisrael or in Sura and Pumbedisa for resolution. The extratalmudic halachic works that do exist (e.g., the *Mechilta* or *Toras Kohanim*) will be discussed in Part III.

7

The Responsa of the *Geonim*

As noted, halachic literature begins with the era of the *geonim,* i.e., after the final editing of the Talmud *Bavli* by the *rabbanan savoraim*. The yeshivos in Sura and Pumbedisa became the spiritual centers for all of Jewry, and questions were addressed to them from all over the world. Many of these questions and the answers that were sent back have appeared in various collections of gaonic responsa. Indeed, some of the works cited below (e.g., the *Seder* of Rav Amram *Gaon* and the *Iggeres* of R. Sherira) are, in fact, responses to specific questions addressed to these *geonim* in their positions as heads of the Babylonian yeshivahs.

In reviewing the literature of the *geonim,* the following works should be noted:

7.1 *Sheiltos* of Rav Achai

Halachic work by R. Achai of Shabcha (8th century). According to the *Iggeres* of R. Sherira, R. Achai was worthy of being appointed *Gaon* of the yeshivah in Pumbedisa. When his student R. Natronai was appointed to the post by the exilarch, Shlomo ben Chasdai, R. Achai left Bavel and moved to Eretz Yisrael.

The *Sheiltos* (literally, questions) combines both halachic and aggadic materials arranged according to the weekly *sidrah,* although the material in each portion is not necessarily directly related to laws mentioned in the *parashah.* Thus, the author discusses the laws of theft in *parashas Noach,* and the laws of mourning in *parashas Vayechi.* R. Achai was a contemporary of R. Yehudai *Gaon* (see 7.2), and their works are the two earliest examples of halachic literature that have come down to us.

7.1.1 ***Sheilas Shalom*** Commentary to the *Sheiltos* by R. Yeshayahu Pick (see 4.7).

7.1.2 ***ha-Amek She'elah*** Commentary to the *Sheiltos* by R. Naftali Tzvi Yehudah Berlin (1817–1893). *Rosh yeshivah* of Volozhin for almost forty years, the *Netziv* (an acrostic of the letters of his Hebrew name) also wrote extensive commentaries to the *Sifri* (*Emek ha-Netziv*), to the Bible (*ha-Amek Davar* and *Harchev Davar*), to *Shir ha-Shirim* (*Rinah shel Torah,* with an essay on the roots of anti-Semitism entitled *She'ar Yisrael*), to the Pesach *haggadah* (*Imrei Shefer*) and responsa (*Meishiv Davar*).

7.2 *Halachos Pesukos*

Halachic work by R. Yehudai ben R. Nachman (8th century) who served as *Gaon/rosh yeshivah* of Sura in the years 757–761. According to the *Iggeres* of Rav Sherira, R. Yehudai was a member of the yeshivah in Pumbedisa, where his brother R. Dudai served as *Gaon.* Although it was unusual for someone who had not studied in Sura to be appointed *Gaon* of that yeshivah, R. Yehudai's scholarship was so great that an exception was made in his case. His work, written originally in Arabic, is often quoted by Tosafos and other *rishonim.*

7.3 *Halachos Gedolos*

Halachic work by R. Shimon Kayara (8th century). R. Shimon is often referred to as the *Ba'al* (author of) *Halachas Gedolos,* or *Bahag* for short, and the work is often quoted by the *rishonim.* In *Halachos Gedolos,* R. Shimon quotes both the *Sheiltos* and the *Halachos Pesukos.*

The *Halachos Gedolos* is, in many ways, the forerunner of later halachic codes for it follows the order of the Talmud and groups the *halachos* that are to be found in various tractates according to their logical order. In his introduction, R. Shimon included a list of the 613 precepts that the Talmud mentions but does not specify—the earliest delineation of the precepts that we have. This listing was severely criticized by the Rambam in his introduction to his *Sefer ha-Mitzvos* and was defended by the Ramban.

7.4 *Seder* of Rav Amram *Gaon*

Responsa of R. Amram (9th century) who served as head of the academy of Sura. During his tenure, R. Yitzchok ben R. Shimon, one of the leaders of the Jewish community in Spain, sent a generous contribution to the yeshivah along with a request asking about the order of the prayers. R. Amram's response is, in essence, the first written *siddur* and includes the *halachos* relevant to prayers. The manuscript was first published in 1865 by R. Nachman Noson Koronel.

7.5 *Aruch*

R. Tzemach bar R. Poltoi (9th century), *Gaon* of Pumbedisa and great-grandfather of R. Sherira *Gaon,* received a request to translate several Aramaic words in the Talmud. Arabic had become the primary language of the Jews in the Moslem countries, and as a result, they were unfamiliar with the language of the Talmud. R. Tzemach sent back a list of translated words, calling this first talmudic dictionary *Aruch* (arranged). Later, R. Nasan ben R. Yechiel of Rome (1035–1106) expanded the list into the first dictionary of talmudic Aramaic. His work was called *Aruch ha-Shalem,* but is more widely known—and quoted—as the *Aruch*.

7.6 *Iggeres* of Rav Sherira *Gaon*

Letter written by R. Sherira (906–1006), *Gaon* of the yeshivah at Pumbedisa, in response to a question addressed to him by the Jewish community of Kairouan, North Africa. In this lengthy epistle, R. Sherira provides us with a record of the transmission of the tradition from the period of the Mishnah through his time; it is often our only source of information about the development of *halachah* in the yeshivos of Bavel and Eretz Yisrael.

8

The *Rif*

The most important example of early halachic literature is the halachic commentary to the Talmud by R. Yitzchok Alfassi (1013–1103). A disciple of Rabbenu Chananel (see 1.3) at the yeshivah in Kairouan, R. Yitzchok established an academy in Fez, Morocco (hence his surname), but was forced to flee to Spain in 1088. He settled first in Cordova and later moved to Lucena where the yeshivah that he established became the primary Torah center for Spain.

His major work, entitled the *Hilchos* of *Rav Alfas* (commonly referred to as the *Rif*), is a summation of the halachic material in the Talmud. The Rif only quotes that portion of the talmudic dialogue that is pertinent today, omitting all *halachos* that are no longer relevant after the destruction of the second *Beis ha-Mikdash,* e.g., the first seven chapters of tractate *Yoma* that deal with the sacrificial service. Unlike earlier halachic works, the Rif does at times refer to the aggadic material in the Talmud, primarily as a means of stressing the importance of a specific *halachah.* His compilation—which is extant to the orders of *Mo'ed, Nashim,* and *Nezikin* as well as to the tractates *Berachos* and *Chullin*—is one of the three works upon which R. Yosef Caro (see chap. 11) based his *Shulchan Aruch.* Among the Rif's most important

רש"י

(*°) היה רוכב ע"ג בהמה וראה את המציאה ואמר לחבירו תנה לי נטלה ואמר לו אני זכיתי בה זכה בה ואם משנתנה לו אמר אני זכיתי בה תחלה לא אמר כלום: גמ' א"ר חייא בר אבא א"ר יוחנן המגביה מציא' לחבירו קנה חבירו וא"ת משנתנו ה"ל תנה לי ולא אמר [ליה] זכה לי: מתני' ראה את המציאה ונפל לו עליה ובא אחר והחזיק בה זה שהחזיק בה זכה (א): ראה אותן רצין אחר המציאה אחר צבי שבור אחר גוזלות שלא פרחו ואמר זכתה לי שדי זכתה לו היה צבי רץ כדרכו וגוזלות מפריחין ואמר זכתה לי שדי לא אמר כלום: גמ' אמר ריש לקיש משום אבא כהן ברדלא ארבע אמות של אדם קונות לו בכל מקום מ"ט תקינו להו רבנן כי היכי דלא ליתו לאינצויי וכל מקום דקאמרינן לאו כל מקום ממש אלא בשדה דעלמא אי נמי בסימטא אי נמי בצידי רה"ר דלא דחקי רבים בהו אבל ברה"ר דדחקי רבים בהו אי נמי בשדה חבירו לא קנו ליה ארבע אמות דיליה: ואמר ר"ל משום אבא כהן ברדלא קטנה אין לה חצר ואין לה ארבע אמות ור' יוחנן משום ר' ינאי אמר יש לה חצר ויש לה ארבע אמות והלכתא קטנה יש לה חצר ויש לה ד' אמות אבל קטן אין לו חצר ואין לו ארבע אמות (ס) [דף סו ע"א] וחצר

גרסינן

The *Rif*

disciples were R. Yosef ha-Levi Ibn mi-Gash (the Ri mi-Gash) and R. Yehudah ha-Levi (author of the *Kuzari*—see 16.3).

The student should note that the commentary of Rashi that is printed alongside the Rif is not a commentary on the Rif—for Rashi was a contemporary of R. Yitzchok Alfassi, and it is highly unlikely that he ever saw the Rif's work—but rather is excerpted from Rashi's commentary to the Talmud. It often differs from the commentary printed alongside the Talmud and may well have been taken from early editions of Rashi. In any event, it is considered to be inaccurate.

Although the Rif usually follows the structure and wording of the Talmud, on occasion the commentary may digress from the talmudic discussion and quote materials from other tractates that are relevant to the subject. For example, the Talmud (*Bava Metzia* 31a) refers in passing to the law requiring one to admonish a friend who has transgressed. The Rif in his commentary cites this *halachah* and proceeds to expand the discussion by citing related *halachos* mentioned in other tractates.

The commentary of the Rif was originally published according to *simanim*—chapters—that are based on each *halachah* introduced by the Talmud. The Rif considered *Bava Kamma, Bava Metzia,* and *Bava Basra* to be one tractate; thus his commentary to *Bava Kamma* begins from *siman* א, the commentary to *Bava Metzia* begins with *siman* רל"ו, and that to *Bava Basra* begins with *siman* תקצ"ט. Later editions found the Rif printed as a sort of mini-Talmud, following the same page layout as the Talmud itself. To enable the student to find the relevant folio number of the Talmud within the Rif's commentary, most publishers have included these numbers in the inside margin alongside the text.

In trying to fathom the immense contribution that the Rif made to the study of *halachah* as well as the impact and influence that his commentary had upon all subsequent literature, the following comments from the Rambam's Introduction to the Mishnah should be noted:

> The *halachos* which the great rabbi R.Yitzchok wrote are greater than all the other works [i.e., those of the *geonim*], for they include all of the principles and laws necessary in our times . . . and he elucidated all of the errors which had been made previously and there are no more than ten instances in which one can disagree with him.

As the first major halachic commentary to the Talmud, the Rif's work generated a number of supercommentaries that are often included in the published editions appended to the Talmud. These include:

8.1 *Hasagos ha-Ra'avad*

Glosses to the Rif by R. Avraham ben Dovid of Posquires (Ra'avad, France—1120–1198). Acknowledged as the primary Torah scholar of Southern France, the Ra'avad defends the commentary of the Rif from the critique offered by his contemporary, R. Zerachiah ha-Levi (the *Ba'al ha-Maor*), although he does, at times, add his own criticism.

8.2 *Meah Shearim*

Notes to the Rif by R.Yitzchok ben Abba Mari of Marseilles (France—1122–1293). A contemporary of the Ra'avad and Rabbenu Tam (with whom he maintained an extensive halachic correspondence), R.Yitzchok also wrote a halachic work known as *Sefer ha-Ittur* that is often cited by later authorities.

8.3 *ha-Maor*

Critical commentary by R. Zerachiah ha-Levi of Provence (France—1125–1186). R. Zerachiah's work is published under two titles: *ha-Maor ha-Gadol* on *Nashim* and *Nezikin,* and *ha-Maor ha-Katan* on *Mo'ed, Berachos,* and *Chullin.* R. Zerachiah was not yet twenty when he wrote his work, and in his introduction he notes that he only proceeded to criticize the work of the Rif because of the great respect that he bore for it. He writes:

> There is no work as beautiful since the sealing of the Talmud, and it is therefore incumbent upon us to beautify it and honor it and clarify it according to our abilities.

8.4 *Rabbenu Yehonasan*

Explanatory commentary to the Rif on tractate *Eruvin* by R. Yehonasan ben David ha-Kohen of Lunel (France—d. 1190). A disciple of the Ra'avad, R. Yehonasan was one of the sages of Lunel who maintained an extensive halachic correspondence with the Rambam. He arranged for R. Shmuel Ibn Tibbon to translate the *Moreh Nevuchim* (see 16.4) into Hebrew from the Arabic original.

8.5 *Milchemes Hashem* and *Sefer ha-Zechus*

A defense of the Rif's work by the Ramban (see 3.1). In the former, the Ramban answers the criticisms offered by R. Zerachiah, and in the latter, he answers the criticisms of the Ra'avad. The Ramban also wrote *Sefer ha-Tashlum* in which he cites the *halachos* pertaining to the firstborn and to the separation of *challah* that, for reasons unknown to us, the Rif omitted.

8.6 *Rabbenu Yonah*

Explanatory commentary to the Rif on tractate *Berachos* by R. Yonah of Gerona (see 16.5).

8.7 *Ran*

Explanatory commentary to the Rif on fourteen tractates by R. Nissim ben Reuven of Gerona (see 3.5).

8.8 *Nimukei Yosef*

Explanatory commentary to the Rif on seven tractates by R.Yosef Chaviva (Spain—15th century). A disciple of R.Nissim and R.Chasdai Crescas, R.Yosef often quotes the works of other *rishonim*—including the Ritva, the *Tur* of R.Yaakov ben Asher, and the *Maggid Mishnah*.

8.9 *Shiltei ha-Gibborim*

Glosses to the Rif by R.Yehoshua Boaz (see 1.4).

9

The *Yad ha-Chazakah*

As noted, the Rif followed the format of the Talmud and only included those *halachos* that were relevant in the period following the destruction of the second *Beis ha-Mikdash*. While the work of the Rif can be seen as a compendium of *halachah,* its structure precluded its use as a code of law that a student or scholar could easily consult to determine the proper practice in a given situation. To be sure, there were codicils that were written both prior to the Rif and in his era, e.g., the *Seder* of Rav Amram *Gaon* that elucidates the *halachos* relevant to the prayer service or the *takkanos* of Rabbenu Gershom. However, there was no single work that encompassed the entire body of *halachah* nor that provided the student/reader with a systematic presentation of *halachah* itself.

The lack of such a work was first addressed by R. Moshe ben Maimon (b. Cordova, 1135, d. Egypt, 1204) in his *Yad ha-Chazakah*. Departing from the custom of the Rif who, in essence, rewrote the Talmud as a halachic work, the Rambam set out to create an entirely new format for *halachah*. In the introduction to the *Yad,* he writes:

> And in this era, we are faced with many troubles and have little time and we have lost the wisdom of our sages and the understanding of our wise

הממכר כמו שביארנו כך הנותן. כיצד הכותב לחבירו קרקע מנכסי נתתה לך. או שכתב לו כל נכסי קניין לך חוץ ממקצתן. הואיל ולא סיים הדבר שנתן לו ואינו ידוע לא קנה כלום. ואינו יכול לומר לו תן לי פחות שבנכסיך עד שסיים לו המקום שנתן לו. אבל אם *אמר לו חלק כך וכך בשדה פלונית הואיל וסיים השדה אע"פ שלא סיים החלק נוטל אותו חלק מן הפחות שבאותה שדה:

ו [א]כל הנותן מתנה על תנאי. בין שהתנה נותן בין שהתנה המקבל והחזיק המקבל וזכה בה. אם נתקיים התנאי נתקיימה המתנה ואם לא נתקיים התנאי בטלה המתנה ויחזיר פירות שאכל. והוא שיהיה התנאי כראוי:

ז [ב]כבר ביארנו שכל תנאין שיש במתנות או במקח וממכר צריך שיהיה תנאי כפול. והן קודם ללאו. והתנאי קודם למעשה. ויהיה תנאי שאפשר לקיימו. ואם חסר אחד מאלו התנאין בטל וכאילו אין שם תנאי:

ח וכל האומר על מנת כאומר מעכשיו דמי ואינו צריך [ג] לכפול התנאי. כך הורו מקצת הגאונים ולזה דעתי נוטה. ורבותי הורו שאין צריך לכפול התנאי ולהקדים הן ללאו אלא בגיטין ובקידושין בלבד

א סמ"ג עשין סי' פב טוח"מ סי' רמא: ב סמ"ג שם טור שם: ג עיין כתוב סי' רמא וכסמ"ג דף קמא ע"ד:

השגת הראב"ד

לחם משנה

לחם משנה

הגהות מיימוניות

מגדל עוז

From the Rambam

men is hidden. Hence, those commentaries, *halachos* and responsa of the *geonim* which they saw as being clear, are difficult in our day and there are few who understand them fully. And it goes without saying [that this is true] of the Talmud *Bavli* and *Yerushalmi*. . . . It is because of this that I, Moses ben Maimon the *Sephardi*, have gathered my strength and have rested upon the Rock, may He be blessed, and I have studied all of these works and have seen fit to write things which are clear from all of these sources regarding that which is permitted and that which is prohibited, that which is pure and that which is impure as well as all of the laws of the Torah.

The Rambam entitled his code *Yad ha-Chazakah* based on the last verse in *Devarim*. Additionally, the word *yad* has a numerical value of fourteen, which alludes to the fourteen separate headings the Rambam used to divide his work (see Appendix II). The Rambam began writing the *Yad* when he was thirty-six and completed it ten years later. Unlike his other works (e.g., *Moreh Nevuchim* or the commentary to the Mishnah), the *Yad* was written in Hebrew rather than in Arabic.

It should be noted that the publication of the *Yad* did not meet with universal approval. The Rambam's groundbreaking approach was criticized by many who saw it as a dangerous precedent in that it would allow readers to study *halachah* without being acquainted with the Talmud. Additionally, the Rambam was severely criticized for not citing sources for his rulings—a failing that was addressed by many of the commentaries that were subsequently written to the work. Yet even the most severe critic of his approach—the Ra'avad—writes that he (the Rambam) did a great thing. The Ramban, who took exception to the Rambam's compilation of the *mitzvos* and who often takes him to task for disregarding the earlier compilation of R. Shimon Kayara (see 7.3 above) writes: "This sainted man—in all of the diaspora of France and Spain there is none who is like him."

The esteem in which the Rambam's *Yad ha-Chazakah* is held can, perhaps, best be seen by the fact that after the Talmud itself, there is probably no other work of Jewish literature that has elicited as much commentary. Indeed, the Rambam's choice of terminology and phrase was considered to be so precise that nuances and halachic derivations are often drawn from his method of expression. We find that the controversy surrounding the renewal of *semichah*—ordination—some 350 years after his passing was based primarily on diverse interpretations of the Rambam's ruling in *Hilchos Sanhedrin* 4:11.

The following commentaries are usually printed alongside the text of the *Yad ha-Chazakah*:

9.1 *Ra'avad*

Critical glosses by R. Avraham ben Dovid of Posquires (see 8.1). The glosses of the Ra'avad are usually cryptic and often seem to cynically disagree with the Rambam's halachic ruling. The Ra'avad's remarks, printed in the margin next to the specific *halachah* with which he disagrees, always begin with the abbreviation א"א—אמר אברהם—Avraham said. Despite the evident sarcasm that the Ra'avad expresses, he held the Rambam in high esteem. It would seem that the feeling was mutual; the Rambam is quoted by *Sefer Tashbatz* (R. Shimon ben Tzemach Duran) to have remarked about the Ra'avad:

> The only person to have bested me was the man of single occupation [i.e., the one who studied Torah without ever having pursued secular knowledge as well].

9.2 *Hagaos Maimonis*

A compendium of sources and cross-references by R. Meir ha-Kohen of Ruttenberg (13th-century France), a disciple of the Maharam of Ruttenberg and brother-in-law of the Mordechai (see 2.10).

9.3 *Migdal Oz*

Defense of the Rambam's opinions in the face of the glosses of the Ra'avad by R. Shemtov Ibn Gaon (late 13th- to early 14th-century Spain). In his *Migdal Oz*, R. Shemtov also provides sources for the Rambam's rulings. The work is extant only on six of the fourteen divisions of the *Yad*.

9.4 *Maggid Mishnah*

Explanatory commentary by R. Vidal Yom Tov (14th-century Spain). A colleague of the Ran, the *Maggid Mishnah* often deals with the questions raised by the Ra'avad and defends the Rambam's position.

9.5 *Radvaz*

Explanatory commentary by R. Dovid ben Zimra (b. Spain—1480, d. Tzefas—1574). Forced to flee Spain in the wake of the Inquisition, R. Dovid established a yeshivah in Cairo where R. Betzalel Ashkenazi (see 3.7) and R. Yitzchok Luria (the *Ari ha-Kadosh*) were his students. The Radvaz wrote a commentary to those sections of the Rambam that were not covered by the *Maggid Mishnah*.

9.6 *Kessef Mishnah*

Explanatory commentary by R. Yosef Caro (chap. 11).

9.7 *Lechem Mishnah*

Explanatory commentary by R. Avraham di-Boton (Salonika—1560–1606).

9.8 *Mishneh la-Melech*

Explanatory commentary by R. Yehudah Rosanes (Constantinople—1657–1727). R. Yehudah, as rabbi of the city, was instrumental in issuing the ban proclaimed against the followers of Shabbetai Tzvi. His commentary to the Rambam was published by his disciple, R. Yaakov Culi—author of *Me'am Loez*.

10

The *Arba'ah Turim*

The publication of the Rambam's *Yad ha-Chazakah* was a momentous event in the history of halachic literature for, as we have seen, the work was the first all-encompassing guide to practice and requirement rather than a halachic synopsis of the Talmud's dialogue.

In the period that followed its publication, a great deal of controversy surrounded the question of accepting the Rambam's halachic decisions as binding. As noted, the Rambam did not cite sources for his rulings—neither from the Talmud nor the responsa of the *geonim* nor the halachic writings of the Rif and others who preceded him.

The Ra'avad, the most implacable opponent of the *Yad,* wrote in his glosses to the introduction to the *Yad:*

> He [the Rambam] thought that he was correcting a situation, but he did not correct it at all, for he abandoned the way charted by all other writers who preceded him. They brought corroboration for their words and quoted things in the name of those who had said them. There was great purpose in doing this, for often a judge feels that he should either permit or prohibit something and his basis for doing so may be from [a deduction or inference from] a certain point. But were he [the judge] to know that

> someone greater than he held differently, then he would very likely retract. And now, I do not see why I should retract from the traditions that I have received or from the evidence that I have drawn because of this work. If the one who wrote it is greater than I, good. But if I am greater than he, why should I retract my opinions because of him? Moreover, there are matters in which the *geonim* differ with each other and this author has chosen the opinion of one and has written them in his work. Why should I rely on his choice when it does not seem correct to me and I do not know who differs with him and whether he is even worthy of disagreeing.

The Ra'avad's criticism of the *Yad*—while not detracting from the esteem with which the work was greeted throughout the Jewish world—seems to have made a strong impression on those sages who chose to write on halachic subjects. In the generations immediately following the Rambam's passing, we find no authors who chose to address the entire body of halachic practice as a separate subject. Although a number of purely halachic works were indeed authored—e.g., *Sefer ha-Manhig* of R. Avraham ben Nasan (1155–1215), *Sefer ha-Rokeach* of R. Eliezer of Worms (1160–1237), *Toras ha-Bayis* of R. Shlomo ben Aderes (see 12.6.), *Orchos Chaim* of R. Aharon ha-Kohen of Lunel (late 13th to early 14th century), and *Kaftor va-Pherach* of R. Eshtori ha-Parchi (1280–1355)—all of these were subject specific rather than covering the entire body of *halachah*.

The next attempt to create a work that would cover every facet of practical *halachah* was undertaken by R. Asher ben Yechiel (the Rosh—see 2.2). In his work, the Rosh returned to the style of the Rif by offering a synopsis of the Talmud. In a sense, the Rosh can be seen as an update of the Rif, for the author adds the *halachos* and opinions of the rabbis who had been active in the years after the Rif's passing. The work of the Rosh, however, did not address the problem that the Rambam had sought to solve in his *Yad*, for its use presupposed mastery of

ב״י חשן המשפט הלכות עדות כט ל ב״ח מד

כל דבר שיאמר העד אחר שנחקר עדותו שבא מכללו ביטול העדות או תוספת תנאי אין שומעין לו וא״א הרא״ש ז״ל כתב דבתנאי שומעין לו ואפילו אחד אומר תנאי ואחד אומר לא היה תנאי שומעין לזה שאומר תנאי ורב מתתיה גאון כתב ואע״פ דעד אחד אומר תנאי ואחד אומר לא היה תנאי קיימא לן דהאומר תנאי נאמן כיון דאיכא רב נחמן דמחייב שבועה והתקן היסת מישתבע ליה היסת דתנאי הוה וסיפור:

ל (א) אין צריך לדרוש עדי ממונות בדרישה וחקירה בין עדי הודאות והלואות בין עדי ירושות מתנות ותולות חוץ מעדי חבלות כיצד אמרו בפנינו הלוה פלוני מנה לפלוני בשנה פלוני אע״פ שלא כיונו החדש שהלוה בו ולא המקום ולא המנה אם

ל (א) אין צריך לדרוש עדי ממונות וכו׳ משנה בסנהדרין (דף לב׳) אחד דיני ממונות ואחד דיני נפשות בדרישה וחקירה שנאמר משפט אחד יהיה לכם ורמינהו עלה מדתניא דדיני ממונות לא בעי דרישה וחקירה ׳ ואמר רבי חנינא דבר תורה אחד דיני ממונות ואחד דיני נפשות בדרישה וחקירה ומ״ט אמרו דיני ממונות לא בעו דרישה וחקירה כדי שלא תנעול דלת בפני לוין ׳ ומתניתין דאורייתא וברייתא דרבנן ורבא אמר תרדייהו בתר תקנתא דרבנן ומתניתין בדיני קנסות

דרכי משה

חדושי הגהות

The *Tur*

the Talmud and could not be used as a source for determining *halachah* in and of itself.

It was only with the publication of the *Arba'ah Turim* of R.Yaakov ben Asher, the son of the Rosh (1280–1340), that the challenge that the Rambam had sought to meet was again addressed. Unlike his father, R. Yaakov abandoned the style of the Rif and followed that of the Rambam, arranging *halachah* systematically rather than according to the Talmud. Unlike the Rambam, however, R.Yaakov provided sources for all of his rulings, quoting extensively from the Talmud and the works of the *geonim* and *rishonim*. He also followed the style of both his father and the Rif by omitting those *halachos* that had no practical application in the period following the destruction of the second *Beis ha-Mikdash*.

R.Yaakov divided his work into four separate books—hence the name *Arba'ah Turim* after the four rows of stones on the breastplate worn by the *kohen gadol* who was consulted to answer questions (see *Shemos* 28:17). He named these divisions *Orach Chaim, Yoreh De'ah, Choshen Mishpat,* and *Even ha-Ezer*. The *Arba'ah Turim* of R.Yaakov—also known as the *Tur*—became the basis for all subsequent halachic writing, and it is his division of the *halachah*—rather than that of the Rambam—that is followed.

The *Tur* won acceptance among most Jewish communities as the authoritative code of *halachah* and is the subject of the following supercommentaries:

10.1 *Beis Yosef*

Commentary on the *Tur* by R.Yosef Caro (see chap. 11). R.Yosef clarifies the opinions quoted by the Tur as well as citing the opinions of authorities who lived after R.Yaakov. R.Yosef spent twenty years compiling the *Beis Yosef* and added a supplement—*Bedek ha-Bayis*—which publishers later incorporated into the commentary itself. In his introduction to the commentary, R. Yosef cites some thirty sources that he used in his work. The *Beis Yosef* should be seen as a complete version of the author's later work—the *Shulchan Aruch* (see chap. 11). R. Yosef compiles the variant opinions cited in the *Tur* and proceeds to render a halachic decision.

In the introduction, he also notes the method that he established in reaching a halachic decision. He based himself on three primary sources: the Rif, the Rambam, and the Rosh. When all three are in agreement, the matter is established as *halachah*. In cases of disagreement, he followed the majority opinion.

10.2 *Bach*

Commentary to the *Tur* by R. Yoel Sirkes (Poland—1561–1640). R. Yoel served as rabbi in Belz, Brisk, and Cracow, where he headed the yeshivah. Among his notable students there was his son-in-law, R. Dovid ben Shmuel ha-Levi—author of the *Taz* (see 11.4). In his commentary, which he called *Bayis Chadash* (abbreviated as *Bach*—the name by which he is widely known), R. Yoel traces the source of the rulings brought by the *Tur*.

10.3 *Darkei Moshe*

Glosses to the *Tur* and *Beis Yosef* by R. Moshe Isserles (see 11.1). R. Moshe added the opinions and customs of Ashkenazic Jewry to complement the materials of both the *Tur* and *Beis Yosef*, which reflected the customs and decisions of Sephardic Jewry.

10.4 *Prisha* and *Drisha*

Glosses to the *Tur* by R. Yehoshua Falk (Poland—1555–1614). A student of R. Moshe Isserles and R. Shlomo Luria (Maharshal—see 12.9),

R.Yehoshua refused to accept rabbinical office, preferring to devote his life to teaching at his yeshivah in Lemberg. Despite the fact that he did not hold communal office, he was a widely respected halachist and was a signatory to many of the enactments of the Council of Four Lands. The *Prisha* and *Drisha* are critical glosses to both the *Tur* and *Beis Yosef* with which R.Yehoshua found fault in that they presented the *halachah* in a manner that enabled people to establish rulings without being completely familiar with the sources—a situation that he felt could lead to erroneous decisions.

11

The *Shulchan Aruch*

With the publication of the *Arba'ah Turim,* the foundation had been laid for a purely halachic work that would enable the student/reader to determine *halachah* without having to wade through all of the voluminous and complex literature of the Talmud. However, the format of the *Tur*—despite the systematic arrangement that had been employed—still presented a number of problems, for it was not a work that was easily consulted in determining the answer to a specific question. In resolving the difficulties presented by the Rambam's code of law—the lack of sources on which the author had based his decision—the *Tur* sacrificed the clarity that the *Yad ha-Chazakah* had provided.

R. Yosef Caro (b. Spain—1488, d. Tzefas—1575), having completed his work on the *Tur* (see 10.1), set out to solve this problem and wrote the *Shulchan Aruch*—literally, the prepared table—as a concise collection of the *halachos* brought in his *Beis Yosef.* As a digest of the more complete *Beis Yosef,* the *Shulchan Aruch* could not be subjected to the criticism that had accompanied the publication of the *Yad ha-Chazakah,* for the sources for his rulings as well as divergent opinions were covered in his more extensive work on the *Tur.* In his introduction, R. Yosef made it clear that he intended the *Shulchan Aruch* to serve as

מאירת עינים חושן משפט לד הלכות עדות שפתי כהן נז באר הגולה

ו סו (ז) ס טבח סז (ט) שיצאתה :) נבילה או טריפה מתחת ידו פסול לעדות

ז [ס] (י) סמז] גנב וכן גזלן פסולים לעדות מעת שגנב או גזל יח (ס) ב) ואע״פ [ז] שהחזירו *[ס] עד שיעשו תשובה

Shulchan Aruch

a guide for the layman. The work has become the cornerstone of *halachah* ever since its publication, supplanting both the *Yad* and the *Tur.* Its popularity is evidenced by the fact that with its publication, R.Yosef is referred to simply as the *mechaber*—the author.

Forced to leave Spain in 1492, R.Yosef Caro settled in Adrianople where he studied in the yeshivah of the kabbalist R.Shlomo Molcho and with R. Shlomo Alkabetz—author of *Lecha Dodi.* In 1536 he moved to Tzefas and was one of the four rabbis ordained by R.Yaakov Beirav. He succeeded R.Yaakov as head of the *beis din* in Tzefas and headed a yeshivah there, among whose students were R.Moshe Alshich and R.Moshe Cordovero. He was a contemporary of R.Moshe di-Trani (the *Mabit*) with whom he differed on various halachic questions.

The *Shulchan Aruch*—which follows the divisions of material established by the *Tur*—was first published in 1564 in Venice. It would seem that R.Yosef actively solicited the comments of R.Moshe Isserles (see 11.1), for the next edition of the *Shulchan Aruch* was published in Cracow in 1569. We do know that the two rabbis maintained close contact; R. Moshe wrote a *sefer* Torah based on a manuscript that R.Yosef sent to him from Israel. The combination of the *Shulchan Aruch* of R.Yosef Caro with the glosses of R. Moshe Isserles has provided Jewry with the authoritative and universally accepted guide to *halachah* that is followed and studied to this day.

In writing the *Shulchan Aruch,* R.Yosef followed the chapter divisions of the *Tur.* However, to enable the reader to quickly locate a specific *halachah* within a section, paragraphs were added so that each *halachah* stood on its own. Thus, while the *Tur* deals with all of the laws of cooking on *Shabbos,* for example, in section 318 in *Orach Chaim,* the *Shulchan Aruch* divides that section into nineteen separate *halachos.* For reference purposes, *halachos* in the *Tur* are referred to by section while *halachos* in *Shulchan Aruch* are referred to by section and paragraph.

The *Shulchan Aruch* elicited a vast amount of commentary, including these major works:

11.1 *Rama*

Glosses by R. Moshe Isserles (Cracow—1525–1572) in which the author cites the prevailing practices of Ashkenazic Jewry whenever they differ from the practices of Sephardic Jewry. R. Moshe took particular exception to R. Yosef Caro's reliance on the Rif and the Rambam when they differed from the Rosh.

The short comments of the Rama (an acronym for R. Moshe Isserles) are incorporated into the body of the *Shulchan Aruch* itself and are printed in Rashi script beginning with the word הגה—correction. In his comments, which he referred to as the *mapah*—tablecloth—R. Moshe does not cite the sources upon which he based his disagreement. It would seem that having written the more extensive *Darkei Moshe* as a commentary to both the *Tur* and the *Beis Yosef,* he did not feel that it was necessary to elaborate.

R. Moshe served as rabbi of Cracow and as head of the yeshivah there. Among his students were R. Dovid Gans (author of the historical work *Tzemach Dovid*), R. Mordechai Jaffe (author of the *Levushim*), R. Avraham Horowitz (father of the *Shelah*), and R. Yehoshua Falk (see 10.4 and 11.2).

Despite his criticisms of the *Shulchan Aruch,* R. Moshe held R. Yosef Caro in the highest esteem. In a responsa he writes: Anyone who argues with him (i.e., R. Yosef Caro) is considered to have argued with the *Shechinah.*

11.2 *Sefer Me'iros Einayim*

Explanatory commentary to *Shulchan Aruch Choshen Mishpat* by R. Yehoshua Falk (see 10.4). In his work (more popularly known by the acronym *S'ma*), R.Yehoshua expands upon the glosses of R. Moshe Isserles. His comments are noted by the insertion of large, square Hebrew letters within the text.

11.3 *Knesses ha-Gedolah*

Commentary to *Shulchan Aruch* by R. Chaim Benvenisti (Turkey—1603–1673). A disciple of R.Yosef di-Trani (*Maharit*), R.Chaim served as rabbi in Smyrna. In his work, he cites the halachic decisions and responsa of the authorities who lived after R.Yosef Caro.

11.4 *Turei Zahav*

Explanatory commentary to *Shulchan Aruch Yoreh De'ah* by R. Dovid ben Shmuel ha-Levi (Poland—1586–1667). R. Dovid was a student at the yeshivah of his father-in-law, R.Yoel Sirkes (the *Bach*—see 10.2), and served as rabbi in Posen and Ostrog. He was forced to flee Poland in the wake of the Chmielnicki uprising in 1648 and settled in Germany. He returned to Poland and in 1654 was appointed rabbi of Lemberg. In the course of his travels, he seems to have spent some time with R. Shabbesai ben Meir ha-Kohen (see 11.5).

R. Dovid wrote a commentary to all four sections of the *Shulchan Aruch,* but his works on *Yoreh De'ah* (known by the acronym *Taz*) and *Orach Chaim* (entitled *Magen David,* the work is also referred to, in conjunction with the *Magen Avraham*, as *Maginei Eretz*) are the most widely known. In his work, R. Dovid often takes exception to the rulings of his contemporary, R. Shabbesai. Familiarity with the arguments of the *Shach* and *Taz,* as they are known, is the basis for being considered a master of *halachah*. The comments of R.Dovid are noted in the text of the *Shulchan Aruch* by the insertion of large, square Hebrew letters within parentheses. The ☛ that sometimes appears within the commentary to *Yoreh De'ah* indicates the introduction of a new concept. In *Orach Chaim,* the symbol is used to indicate explanatory remarks by R. Efraim Zalman Margolios (see 11.8.2).

The importance of R. Dovid's work is best evidenced by the fact that his commentary was itself the subject of later authors; most notably the *Mishbetzos Zahav* of R. Yosef ben Meir Teumim (the *Pri Megadim*—see 11.15).

11.5 *Sifsei Kohen*

Explanatory commentary to *Shulchan Aruch Yoreh De'ah* and *Choshen Mishpat* by R. Shabbesai ben Meir ha-Kohen (b. Poland—1621, d. Moravia—1662). R. Shabbesai was married to a great-granddaughter of the Rama and served as a *dayyan* in Vilna. He was forced to flee from the city during the Chmielnicki uprising; his vivid account of the sufferings of the Jews of Lithuania and Poland are recounted in his *Megillas Eifah*.

His commentary to *Shulchan Aruch Yoreh De'ah* was first published in 1646 and was republished in 1674 together with the *Taz*. R. Shabbesai replied to many of the questions raised by the *Taz* in his *Nekkudas ha-Kessef,* and the responses of his colleague, R. Dovid ha-Levi, were published in the latter's *Daf Acharon*. R. Shabbesai responded to the answers provided by R. Dovid in his *Kunteres Acharon*.

The commentary of R. Shabbesai (popularly referred to as the *Shach*) is noted in the text of *Yoreh De'ah* by large, square Hebrew letters, and in *Choshen Mishpat* by square Hebrew letters in parentheses. The commentary to *Yoreh De'ah* is the subject of a supercommentary by R. Yosef Teumim (the *Pri Megadim*) entitled *Sifsei Da'as*.

11.6 *Chelkas Mechokek*

Commentary to *Shulchan Aruch Even ha-Ezer* by R. Moshe Lima (Poland—1605–1658). R. Moshe was a disciple of R. Yehoshua Falk (see 10.4) and served as rabbi of Slonim, later moving to Vilna where he served as *dayyan* together with R. Shabbesai ha-Kohen. His comments are noted by the insertion of a square Hebrew letter enclosed in parentheses.

In section 17 of *Even ha-Ezer,* R. Moshe added a long treatise entiled *Kunteres ha-Agunos* in which he provides a collection of responsa and commentaries specifying the grounds through which an *agunah* may remarry.

11.7 *Beis Shmuel*

Commentary to *Shulchan Aruch Even ha-Ezer* by R. Shmuel Phoebus (Poland—1650–1700), rabbi of Fuerth, Germany, and later Szydlowicz, Poland. His comments are noted in the text by a large, square Hebrew letter.

11.8 *Magen Avraham*

Commentary to *Shulchan Aruch Orach Chaim* by R. Avraham Abeli Gombiner (1637–1683). R. Avraham served as head of the yeshivah and *dayyan* in Kalisz. His comments are noted by a large, square Hebrew letter.

11.8.1 *Machatzis ha-Shekel* Commentary to the *Magen Avraham* by R. Shmuel ha-Levi Kolin (Bohemia—1720–1806). R. Shmuel's work clarifies the difficulties in the *Magen Avraham* and provides the sources that R. Avraham only alluded to in his work.

11.8.2 *Yad Efraim* Supercommentary to the commentaries of the *Taz* and *Magen Avraham* on *Orach Chaim* by R. Efraim Zalman Margolios (Poland—1760–1828). A disciple of R. Yechezkel Landau, R. Efraim Zalman was a highly successful businessman who spent most of his time studying. His explanatory comments are noted by the symbol ☛ within the text. He also wrote *Beis Efraim* on *Yoreh De'ah,* and *Tiv Gittin*—a compendium of the proper spelling of names critical for the proper issuance of divorce documents. R.Tzvi Hirsh Chayes was his student.

11.9 *Be'er ha-Golah*

Glosses to the entire *Shulchan Aruch* by R. Moshe Rivkes (d. Vilna—1672). R. Moshe provides source references for the rulings of R.Yosef Caro, which are noted by the insertion of a small Rashi script letter within the text. He also corrected the text of the *Shulchan Aruch* published in Amsterdam (1661–1666), and his emendations have been included in all subsequent editions. R. Moshe was an ancestor of R. Eliyahu of Vilna who was supported by a legacy that he left.

11.10 *Pri Chadash*

Critical commentary to the *Shulchan Aruch* by R. Chizkiah de-Silva (b. Italy—1659, d. Jerusalem—1695). A disciple of R. Moshe Galante—head of the *Beis Yaakov* yeshivah in Jerusalem—R. Chizkiah was a vociferous opponent of the views of the *Shulchan Aruch* and the *Tur,* basing his rulings on the Rambam whom he viewed as the unsurpassed codifier. His comments are usually found on the outside margin of the *Shulchan Aruch.*

11.11 *Ba'er Heitev*

Commentary to *Shulchan Aruch Orach Chaim* and *Even ha-Ezer* by R. Yehudah Ashkenazi (Germany—18th century) and on *Shulchan Aruch Yoreh De'ah* and *Choshen Mishpat* by R. Zechariah Mendel of Belz (Poland—second half of 17th century). The commentaries are noted by the insertion of a small letter in Rashi script enclosed in parentheses.

11.12 *Mateh Yehonasan*

Glosses to the *Shulchan Aruch* by R.Yonasan Eybeschutz (b. Cracow—1690, d. Hamburg—1764). R.Yonasan served as rabbi in Prague and later in the three sister communities of Germany: Altona, Wannsbeck, and Hamburg. It was in this latter position that he became embroiled in an acrimonious dispute with R.Yaakov Emden who accused him of writing amulets that suggested an affinity to Shabbetai Tzvi. The controversy raged for many years, and most of the rabbinical figures of Europe tried to reconcile the two parties but to no avail. A gifted orator and writer, R.Yonasan also authored longer halachic works—*Kresi U'Plesi* on *Yoreh De'ah* and *Urim ve-Tumim* on *Choshen Mishpat*—as well as many homiletical works including *Ya'aros D'vash* and *Ahavas Yehonasan*.

11.13 *Dagul Merivava*

Glosses to the *Shulchan Aruch* by R.Yechezkel Landau (b. Poland—1713, d. Prague—1793). R.Yechezkel served as rabbi of Prague and was the outstanding halachist of his era. He also wrote extensive responsa—*Noda b'Yehudah*—as well as a commentary to tractates *Berachos, Pesachim,* and *Betzah* entitled *Tzion le-Nefesh Chayah* (*Tzlach*). His brief notes are usually printed on the outside margin and are marked in the text by an asterisk with a single parenthesis.

11.14 *ha-Gaos ha-Gra*

Glosses to the *Shulchan Aruch* by R. Eliyahu of Vilna (1720–1797). Although he never served in an official capacity, R. Eliyahu was the undisputed leader of Jewry in his era, and his awesome erudition and scholarship led to his being referred to simply as the "*Gaon* of Vilna." Supported by a legacy left by his ancestor, R.Moshe Rivkes (see 11.9), R. Eliyahu spent his entire life involved in study. He was a prolific author and his writings cover almost every field of Torah study. R. Chaim of Volozhin and R.Yisroel of Shklov (author of *P'as ha-Shulchan*) were his disciples. R.Eliyahu's glosses to *Shulchan Aruch* are cryptic and concise and were taken from the marginal notes that he wrote on his own copy.

11.15 *Pri Megadim*

Commentary to *Shulchan Aruch Orach Chaim* and *Yoreh De'ah* by R.Yosef Teumim (Poland—1727–1792). R.Yosef served as rabbi of Frankfurt on the Oder where he stipulated that his acceptance of the position was contingent on the community agreeing to support a small yeshivah.

His commentary to *Yoreh De'ah* included a supercommentary to the *Shach* and *Taz* (*Sifsei Da'as*). He also included an introduction to the laws of forbidden mixtures entitled *Sha'ar ha-Ta'aruvos*. His commentary to *Orach Chaim* included a supercommentary to the *Taz* (entitled *Mishbetzos Zahav*) and to the *Magen Avraham* (entitled *Eshel Avraham*). His works were considered so authoritative that his contemporaries were reported to have declared that "the Heavenly *beis din* also rules according to the *Pri Megadim*."

11.16 *Sha'arei Teshuvah*

Commentary to *Shulchan Aruch Orach Chaim* by R.Chaim Mordechai Margolios (Poland—late 18th century), rabbi of Dubnow. In his commentary, R.Chaim Mordechai cites the opinions brought in the responsa literature. He was a brother of R.Efraim Zalman Margolios (see

11.8.2). His comments are noted by the insertion of a small letter in square script enclosed in parentheses.

11.17 *Ketzos ha-Choshen* and *Avnei Miluim*

Commentaries to *Shulchan Aruch Choshen Mishpat* and *Even ha-Ezer* by R. Aryeh Leib Heller (Poland—1745–1813). A descendant of R. Yom Tov Lipman Heller (see 4.3), R. Aryeh Leib was a student of R. Meshullam Igra (predecessor of R. Moshe Sofer at the yeshivah of Pressburg) and served as head of the yeshivah in Stry, Poland. He also wrote *Shav Shematseh* on the laws pertaining to cases of doubt.

11.18 *Nesivos ha-Mishpat*

Commentary to *Shulchan Aruch Choshen Mishpat* by R. Yaakov Lorberbaum (Poland—1760–1832). A colleague of R. Aryeh Leib Heller at the yeshivah of R. Meshullam Igra, he wrote his *Nesivos ha-Mishpat* as a response to some of the conclusions reached in the *Ketzos ha-Choshen*. R. Yaakov served as rabbi in Kalisz and later served the community in Lissa where he also headed the yeshivah. R. Tzvi Hirsh Kalisher was his student. He joined together with R. Akiva Eiger and R. Moshe Sofer in battling the reform movement in Southeastern Europe. R. Yaakov was the author of *Toras Gittin* on the laws of divorce and *Imrei Yosher*, a commentary to the five *megillos*.

11.19 *ha-Gaos R. Akiva Eiger*

Glosses to the *Shulchan Aruch* by R. Akiva Eiger (see 3.10). R. Akiva was considered to be the outstanding halachic authority of his era, and his glosses provide a concise and sometimes cryptic commentary to the text.

11.20 *Chasam Sofer*

Commentary to the *Shulchan Aruch* by R. Moshe Sofer (b. Bohemia—1762, d. Hungary—1839). R. Moshe was a disciple of R. Pinchas Horowitz (author of the *Hafla'ah*) and R. Noson Adler in Frankfurt. In 1806 he was appointed rabbi of Pressburg and also headed its yeshivah. Under his leadership, the yeshivah grew to become the most significant institution in central and southern Europe, attracting students from many countries. When his first wife died, he married the daughter of R. Akiva Eiger. He was a prolific writer, and his works include extensive responsa, novellae on the Talmud, and a commentary to the Bible, all entitled *Chasam Sofer*. His glosses to *Shulchan Aruch* are usually printed on the outside margin.

11.21 *Pischei Teshuvah*

Commentary to *Shulchan Aruch Yoreh De'ah, Choshen Mishpat,* and *Even ha-Ezer* by R. Avraham Tzvi Eisenstadt (Poland—1813–1868). In his commentary, R. Avraham Tzvi quotes the halachic decisions brought in the responsa literature and relates them to the *Shulchan Aruch*. He did not publish a work on *Orach Chaim* since a similar commentary—*Sha'arei Teshuvah* (see 11.16)—had already been written. The comments are noted by the insertion of a small letter in square script enclosed in parentheses.

11.22 *Levushei Srad*

Commentary to *Shulchan Aruch Orach Chaim* and *Yoreh De'ah* by R. Dovid Shlomo Eibeschutz (Bessarabia—19th century), rabbi in Soroki, Romania. His comments are noted by a superscript $^{\circ}$ enclosed within parentheses.

11.23 *Chochmas Shlomo*

Commentary to the *Shulchan Aruch* by R. Shlomo Kluger (Poland 1785–1869). A student of R. Yaakov Kranz (the *Maggid* of Dubno), R. Shlomo served as rabbi in Brody for almost fifty years. He wrote extensive responsa and was considered to be one of the major halachic authorities of his time, leading the opposition to the introduction of machine-made *matzos*.

12

Early Halachic Literature

As we have briefly noted, a number of halachic works were authored by *rishonim* other than the Rif, Rambam, Rosh, and *Tur.* For the most part, these works were not all inclusive codes of practice like the Rambam or *Tur,* nor were they halachic summations of the Talmud—like the Rif and the Rosh. Rather, they dealt with specific halachic areas or discussed *halachah* within the framework of the *mitzvos* (e.g., the *Sefer Mitzvos Gadol* and the *Sefer ha-Chinuch*). The following entries, which cover the period from the Rif until the publication of the *Shulchan Aruch* with the glosses of the Rama, include works that the student might find mentioned or quoted in the major sources that have been dealt with previously.

12.1 *Machzor Vitri*

Compilation of *halachos* pertaining to prayer throughout the yearly cycle (hence the title *machzor*—cycle) by R. Simchah ben Shmuel (Vitri, France—11th century). The *Machzor Vitri* also includes sections on the *halachos* of *Shabbos, eruv,* marriage, and slaughter; thus, it cannot be seen as a *siddur.*

R. Simchah was a contemporary of Rashi—according to some, he was a disciple—and his rulings reflect Rashi's opinions. His son Shmuel married Rashi's granddaughter; R. Isaac of Dampierre (the Ri) was their son.

A number of versions of the *Machzor Vitri* are extant, with some containing materials omitted by the others. It would appear that later additions were made—especially by the tosafists who quote it extensively (e.g., R. Moshe of Coucy in the *Sefer Mitzvos Gadol* and R. Yitzchok ben Moshe of Vienna in the *Or Zarua*).

12.2 *Sefer ha-Rokeach*

Compilation of *halachos* of *Shabbos,* festivals, *kashrus,* and *teshuvah* by R. Eliezer ben Yehudah of Worms (Germany—1160–1237). R. Eliezer, a disciple of R. Yehudah ha-Chasid and one of the *chasidei Ashkenaz,* lost his wife, daughter, and son during the persecutions that accompanied the Crusades. In his work, he included many *minhagim* that he suggested that people should follow.

12.3 *Sefer Mitzvos Gadol*

A compilation of *halachos* organized according to the *mitzvos* by R. Moshe ben Yaakov of Coucy (France—13th century). He was a disciple of R. Yehudah Gur Aryeh (Judah Sir Leon) of Paris and of his father, who is quoted a number of times in the commentary of Tosafos to the Talmud (e.g., *Kiddushin* 43b, s.v. *t'nan hasam*). R. Moshe was a participant in the debate with the apostate Nicholas Donin that led to the burning of the Talmud in Paris in 1242. (שאלי שרופה באש—one of the *kinos* recited on *Tishah b'Av*—was written as a lamentation to mark this occasion by R. Meir of Ruttenberg, another of the participants.)

The *Sefer Mitzvos Gadol* (known by the acronym *Semag*) follows the basic order of the *mitzvos* that the Rambam used in his introduction to the *Yad ha-Chazakah* and quotes from it extensively. The *Semag,* unlike the Rambam, provides both scriptural and talmudic sources as well as a number of *halachos* that are relevant to specific precepts. At the end of the work, R. Moshe included a section on the *mitzvos* that are rabbinically obligatory.

The *Semag* is itself the subject of many commentaries including a digest of the rulings of R. Moshe entitled *Sefer Mitzvos Katan* (*Semak*) by R. Yitzchok of Corbeill.

12.4 *Toras ha-Adam*

Compilation of the *halachos* relevant to mourning and burial written by the Ramban (see 3.1). The final part of the work—entitled *Sha'ar ha-Gemul*—clarifies many of the most fundamental issues of *hashkafah,* including the concepts of reward and punishment, the immortality of the soul, and *techiyas ha-meisim.*

12.5 *Sefer ha-Chinuch*

Compilation of the 613 precepts of unknown authorship. In the introduction to the work, the author refers to himself as "a Jew from Barcelona from the house of Levi." Some scholars attribute the work to R. Aharon ha-Levi of Barcelona (1235–1300), a disciple of the Ramban and colleague of the Rashba. The *Chinuch* is not the earliest compilation of the 613 precepts; as we have seen, R. Shimon Kayara listed the mitzvos in his *Halachos Gedolos,* as did the Rambam in his *Sefer ha-Mitzvos,* which was written as an introduction to the *Yad ha-Chazakah.* While the classification of the *mitzvos* in the *Sefer ha-Chinuch* usually follows the Rambam—although the Ramban is mentioned in those instances where he took exception to the Rambam—the listing of the *mitzvos* is arranged according to their appearance in the Torah.

The author first offers a short description of the *mitzvah,* followed by a citation of the verse in the Torah where the precept is mentioned.

He then proceeds to cite the talmudic and extratalmudic sources where the *mitzvah* is discussed. He also often offers reasons as to the purpose of the *mitzvah,* provides a brief synopsis of the *halachos* that are obligatory as a result of the *mitzvah,* and specifies who is obligated in the *mitzvah* and whether it is obligatory today.

12.5.1 *Minchas Chinuch* Commentary to the *Sefer ha-Chinuch* by R. Yosef Babad (Poland—1800–1874). In his commentary, R. Yosef cites many additional sources and opinions.

12.6 *Toras ha-Bayis*

Compilation of the *halachos* of *issur ve-heter*—including the laws of ritual slaughter, of *kashrus,* and of *niddah*—written by the Rashba (see 3.2).

Although it is beyond the scope of this work to deal with responsa literature, the following three scholars should be noted, for their opinions and rulings are the basis upon which R. Moshe Isserles (the Rama—see 11.1) differs with R. Yosef Caro in his glosses to the *Shulchan Aruch.*

12.7 *Maharil*

Halachic responsa of R. Yaakov Moellin (Germany 1360–1427).

12.8 *Terumas ha-Deshen*

Halachic responsa of R. Yisrael Isserlein (Germany—1390–1460).

12.9 *Maharshal*

Halachic responsa of R. Shlomo Luria (author of the talmudic commentary *Yam Shel Shlomo*) (Poland— 1510–1573). Although R. Shlomo was a contemporary of R. Moshe Isserles, his extensive responsa serve as one of the primary sources for the development and record of Ashkenazic customs.

13

Later Halachic Literature

The publication of the *Shulchan Aruch* together with the glosses of the Rama provided Jewry with a universally acceptable code of law—one that could be used by both Ashkenazic and Sephardic Jewry. Indeed, once the complete *Shulchan Aruch* was published, we find that it became a source in and of itself, i.e., responsa and halachic literature based their opinions on the rulings of either R.Yosef Caro or R.Moshe Isserles. The thrust of halachic writing was now directed toward explaining the *Shulchan Aruch* as can be seen in the works listed in chapter 11.

For a period of some 200 years, we find no evidence of a need either to update the *Shulchan Aruch* as a code of law or to issue major new halachic works in specific areas of practice. It is beyond our ability to offer the reader a proven reason why this type of literature was again found necessary toward the end of the eighteenth century. We can merely hypothesize that in the aftermath of the Chmielnicki uprising and in the wake of the Shabbatean and Frankist movements, it was decided that it was necessary to provide a clear statement of *halachah* for the benefit of the populace at large. Moreover, the various commentaries written on the *Shulchan Aruch* in the centuries after its publication may have led to a diversity of practice—based on local custom and adherence to the rulings of one commentator rather than another—that threatened the uniformity of practice that is the hallmark of observant Jewry.

We might also conjecture that the founding of *Chasidus* and the reaction of the Jewish establishment to its introduction of new *minhagim* (e.g., in following the practice of the *Ari ha-Kadosh* in prayer or in using honed knives for slaughter) led both sides to see it necessary to issue halachic works that would unequivocally present the *halachah* to their adherents. Indeed, the first two examples that we shall examine represent halachic works of the *chasidim* and *misnagdim* respectively.

13.1 *Shulchan Aruch ha-Rav*

Restatement of the *Shulchan Aruch* by R. Shneur Zalman of Liadi (Russia—1745–1813). According to Chabad tradition, R. Shneur Zalman wrote his *Shulchan Aruch*—which was intended as a guide to halachic practice according to the custom of the *chasidim*—at the express request of his master, R. Dov Baer (the *Maggid* of Mezeritch). Interestingly, the work was never accepted by other chasidic groups.

In 1774, after the death of the *Maggid,* R. Shneur Zalman—accompanied by R. Menachem Mendel of Vitebsk—traveled to Vilna in an attempt to meet with the Vilna *Gaon* and reach an understanding that would put an end to the bitter internecine strife between the two camps, but R. Eliyahu refused to meet with them. In 1798, R. Shneur Zalman was arrested and charged with treason (for transferring funds from Russia to support the chasidic groups that had settled in Eretz Yisrael) and for creating a new sect (a serious crime in Czarist Russia). He was released on the 19th of *Kislev,* a date that is celebrated as a holiday by his followers to this day. R. Shneur Zalman also wrote *Sefer ha-Tanya*—the major exposition of the philosophy of *Chabad Chasidus.*

13.2 *Chayei Adam* and *Chochmas Adam*

Restatement of *Shulchan Aruch Orach Chaim* and *Yoreh De'ah* by R. Avrahom Danzig (Poland—1748–1820). A disciple of R. Yechezkel Landau and *dayyan* in Vilna during the last years of the Vilna *Gaon's* life, R. Avrahom wrote his work as an aid to students and laymen who found the divergent opinions cited in the commentaries on the *Shulchan Aruch* confusing. Although he too cites many different opinions in his work, he offers the reader a clear ruling of the *halachah*.

13.3 *Kitzur Shulchan Aruch*

Concise digest of *halachah* by R. Shlomo Ganzfried (Hungary—1804–1886). R. Shlomo intended his work for use by laymen and therefore did not cite sources for his rulings nor did he include those *halachos* that had no practical application to most people (e.g., the laws of marriage and divorce). R. Shlomo served as *av beis din* in Ungvar and also wrote *Kesses ha-Sofer*—a major work on the laws governing the writing of Torah scrolls, *mezuzos*, and *tefillin*.

The *Kitzur Shulchan Aruch* became an immensely popular work soon after its publication thanks to its clear and precise presentation of *halachah*. It has been updated to include those *halachos* applicable in Eretz Yisrael (e.g., the laws of *terumos* and *ma'asros*) by a number of authors.

13.4 *Aruch ha-Shulchan*

Restatement of the entire *Shulchan Aruch* by R. Yechiel Michel ha-Levi Epstein (Russia—1829–1908). A disciple of R. Yitzchok of Volozhin, R. Yechiel Michel served as rabbi in Novogrudok.

In his introduction to *Choshen Mishpat*, R. Yechiel Michel writes that he undertook the work to update the *Shulchan Aruch* by including those rulings that had been made since its publication. The *Aruch ha-Shulchan* follows the order established in the *Shulchan Aruch,* but the internal presentation is far more elaborate as the author discusses the sources of the *halachah* as well as offering many different opinions before stating his ruling. R.Yechiel Michel also wrote a companion to the *Aruch ha-Shulchan,* entitled *Aruch ha-Shulchan le-Asid* (literally, for the future) in which he included the *halachos* that would only again become obligatory with the coming of *Mashiach.*

13.5 *Mishnah Berurah*

Commentary on *Shulchan Aruch Orach Chaim* by R.Yisroel Meir ha-Kohen (the *Chafetz Chaim;* Poland—1838–1933). Although he never held a formal position as a rabbi or *rosh yeshivah*—supporting himself from the earnings of a grocery store that his wife managed and for which he kept the records—hundreds of students flocked to his modest home in Radin. Eventually, a yeshivah was established—headed by R. Naftali Trop—that R.Yisroel Meir supported.

A prolific writer, R.Yisroel Meir's purpose in his works was to strengthen the level of observance of his fellow Jews. His first work—*Chafetz Chaim* on the laws of *lashon ha-ra*—was published anonymously. He also wrote *Machaneh Yisrael,* a digest of laws and observance for Jewish soldiers; *Ahavas Chesed,* on the laws of charity; and *Nidchei Yisrael,* essays to encourage Jews who had emigrated to the West to maintain their adherence to *halachah.*

The *Mishnah Berurah* has become the authoritative halachic guide for Ashkenazic Jewry. R.Yisroel Meir included a second commentary entitled *Biur Halachah* in which he elaborates on many points brought in the *Mishnah Berurah* as well as *Sha'ar ha-Tziyun,* which provides the sources for his rulings.

13.6 *Chazon Ish*

Halachic commentary to the *Shulchan Aruch* by R. Avrohom Yeshayahu Karelitz (b. Lithuania—1878, d. Israel—1953). The first volume of R. Avrohom Yeshayahu's commentary, entitled *Chazon Ish* (Ish being an acrostic for his Hebrew name) was published anonymously in Vilna in 1911, and the scholarship that it evidenced created a deep impression in the rabbinical world. R. Chaim Ozer Gorodinski, *av beis din* of Vilna, consulted with him often.

In 1933, R. Avrohom Yeshayahu moved to Eretz Yisrael and settled in Bnei Brak. Although he held no official position, he was the most important halachic authority of his era (although a number of his rulings were disputed by others, most notably Chief Rabbi Yitzchak Herzog and R. Tzvi Pesach Frank of Jerusalem).

His halachic commentaries deal with many contemporary issues (e.g., the International Dateline, the use of electricity on *Shabbos,* the use of automatic machinery for milking cows on *Shabbos* and festivals and the permissibility of hydroponic cultivation during *shemittah*). He was considered particularly expert in the *halachos* applicable specifically in Eretz Yisrael.

III
RABBINIC LITERATURE

To this point, we have attempted to give the reader a sample of the major works of talmudic and halachic commentary that he is likely to come across in the course of his studies. In the following section, we shall present some of the other examples of rabbinic literature that cannot be classified under the headings of the first two sections of this work but that are quoted in both the Talmud and *halachah.* With the reader's indulgence, we shall include an eclectic selection, with the various chapters not necessarily dealing with related subject areas.

Outside of *Tanach,* the earliest example of a rabbinical work would probably be the *Sefer Yetzirah,* whose authorship is ascribed to the Patriarch Avraham. Note should also be made of what the Talmud refers to as *seforim chitzoni'im*—literally, outside literature—which date mostly from the period of the second *Beis ha-Mikdash* but were not included in the twenty-four books of *Tanach.* These include the *Sefer ha-Chashmonaim* and *Sefer Ben Sira.*

Other examples of early literature that are sometimes quoted include the historical *Seder Olam* ascribed to the *tanna,* R. Yosi bar Chalafta, and *Megillas Ta'anis,* a historical record of the thirty-six days when fasting is prohibited because of joyous events that transpired. According to the Talmud (*Shabbos* 13b), it was compiled by the *tanna* R. Chananiah ben Chizkiah. The student will also find references to *megillas s'tarim*—concealed scrolls (e.g., *Bava Metzia* 92a). Rashi (s.v. *megillas s'tarim*) explains that these scrolls were hidden because they were composed during the period when it was still prohibited to commit the orally transmitted Torah to writing. They had only been written because the authors were afraid that they might forget the *halachos* dealt with therein; i.e., they were private records not meant for publication or circulation.

Special mention should be made of the historical work by Josephus Flavius (1st century C.E.). It would seem that this work was written by Yosef ben Gurion ha-Kohen (some historians maintain that his father's name was Matisyahu) who served as Jewish commander in the Galil at the time of the destruction of the second *Beis ha-Mikdash*. When his army was defeated, he surrendered to the Romans and accompanied the emperor Vespasian during his siege of Jerusalem. It is not entirely clear if the Yossipon ben Gurion quoted by Rashi (e.g., *Bava Basra* 3b, s.v. *haichi asveih*) is the same work or a later version based on the original. In any case, the work was well known during the period of the *rishonim* and offers valuable historical insights to the period of the Destruction.

14

Targumim

The first recorded translation of the Torah was undertaken by a group of seventy-two scholars whom Ptolemy II Philadelphus (Talmai), Greek ruler of Eretz Yisrael (3rd century B.C.E), gathered in Alexandria, Egypt (see *Megillah* 9a). The Talmud (*Soferim* 1:7) notes that the day when the Torah was translated into Greek was as disastrous for the Jews as the day on which they worshiped the golden calf. Nevertheless, it would seem that despite the evident objections that the sages had to translating the Torah—objections that were based on presenting the Torah in a language other than *lashon ha-kodesh*—there were Aramaic translations of the Torah that predated the Greek version and that were used as educational tools. Thus, we find that the Mishnah (*Megillah* 3:3) refers to the role of the *meturgamen*—the translator—who would translate the Torah reading for the benefit of the congregation. However, it is clear from Rashi (*Bava Basra* 23b, s.v. *velo yikra ha-meturgaman*) that this translation was recited by heart rather than being read from a written version.

The two examples that follow are interpretive Aramaic translations rather than literal in that they include materials that explain the text as well. The student should note that the Talmud, while identifying the authors, makes it clear that they were both based on received traditions.

14.1 *Yonasan ben Uziel*

The Talmud (*Megillah* 3a) ascribes the Aramaic translation of the *Nevi'im* to Yonasan ben Uziel, the greatest of Hillel's students (1st century B.C.E.). His *targum* was based on the tradition that had been passed down from Chagai, Zechariah, and Malachi—the last of the prophets.

Most scholars maintain that authorship of *Targum Yonasan* to the Torah, which appears in the *Mikraos Gedolos* editions, cannot be ascribed to Yonasan ben Uziel. Some conjecture that the mistake may have resulted because someone had labeled the *targum* as ת״י for *Targum Yerushalmi*—whose authorship is unknown—and the abbreviation had been assumed to be for *Targum Yonasan*. The Maharitz Chayes states unequivocally that the *Targum Yerushalmi* was not written by Yonasan, although he does not mention who the real author was.

14.2 *Onkelos*

According to the Talmud (*Megillah* 3a), the Aramaic translation of the Torah was written by Onkelos, the proselyte, according to the teachings of the *tanna'im,* R. Eliezer and R. Yehoshua—the disciples of R. Yochanan ben Zakkai. A nephew of Titus, Onkelos lived at the time of the destruction of the second *Beis ha-Mikdash* (1st century C.E.).

According to the *Yerushalmi* (*Megillah* 1:9), the *Targum* of the Torah was written by Aquilas, the proselyte. While the *Korban Edah* (ad loc.) explains that the reference is to Onkelos, other commentators maintain that the reference is to the Greek translation dating from the time of Ptolemy that was then rendered into Aramaic.

15

Midrash Halachah and *Midrash Aggadah*

In Part IV of this work, we shall elaborate on the methods that the sages used in deriving laws from the Torah and in proving that their rulings were consistent with the Torah's intent. These methods are the subject of many of the discussions of the Mishnah and *gemara* as we have seen. However, there is an additional body of literature that is sometimes quoted in the Talmud or parallels the material brought therein. Generally, we can categorize this as midrashic literature and can divide it into two subject areas: *Midrash halachah,* which are the records of the halachic exegesis of Scripture, and *Midrash aggadah,* which are the ethical and moral teachings that are linked to Scripture. Both of these *midrashim* are integral parts of the orally transmitted Torah.

In his commentary to the Torah (*Shemos* 21:2), R. Samson Rafael Hirsh (Germany—1808–1888) explains that the written Torah can be compared to a notebook written by a student who had heard a lecture; the short, cryptic notes he takes are sufficient to enable him to recall the entire lesson that he had attended. The orally transmitted Torah, on the other hand, gives subsequent generations the ability to understand the lecture by expanding these notes into a form that has meaning.

א"ל לא תאמר לי בן א"א סן בולכיף. כי שם בלל ה' שפת כל הארץ: (יז) וא"ה תולדות תרח תרח הוליד את אברם וגו' ר"א בר אבא כ"כ כל מי שנכפל שמו יש לו חלק לעה"ז ולעה"ב. אתיבון ליה והכתיב אלה תולדות תרח תרח יש לו בעה"ז ויש לו לעה"ב. אתמהא. א"ל אף היא לא תברא דא"ר יודן סמים ר"א כ"ב (בראשית טו) ואתה תבוא אל אבותיך בשלום. בשרו שיש לאביו חלק לעה"ב. תקבר בשיבה טובה. לבשרו שישמעאל עושה תשובה: (יח) וימת הרן על פני תרח אביו. ר' חייא בריה דרב אדא דיפו אמר תרח עובד לצלמים ומוכר היה. חד זמן נפיק לאתר. הושיב לאברהם מוכר תחתיו. הוה אתי בר איניש בעי דיזבן. והוה א"ל בר כמה שנין את. והוה א"ל בר חמשין או שיתין. והוה א"ל ווי ליה להדא גברא דהוא בר שיתין ובעי למסגד לבר יומא. והוה מתבייש והולך לו. חד זמן אתת חדא איתתא טעינא בידה חדא פינך דסולת. א"ל הא לך קריב קדמיהון. קם נסיב בוקלסא בידיה ותברהון לכולהון פסילייא. ויהב בוקלסא בידא דרבה דהוה ביניהון. כיון דאתא אבוה א"ל מאן עביד להון כדין. א"ל מה נכפור מינך. אתת חדא איתתא טעינא לה חדא פינך דסולת. ואמרת לי הא לך קריב קדמיהון. קריבת לקדמיהון. הוה דין אמר אנא איכול קדמאי. ודין אמר אנא איכול קדמאי. קם הדין רבה דהוה ביניהון. נסיב בוקלסא ותברינון. א"ל מה אתה מפלה בי וידעין אינון. א"ל ולא ישמעו אזניך מה שפיך אומר. נסביה ומסריה לנמרוד. א"ל נסגוד לנורא. א"ל אברהם ונסגוד למיא דמטפין נורא. א"ל נמרוד נסגוד למיא. א"ל א"כ נסגוד לעננא דטעין מיא. א"ל נסגוד לעננא. [א"ל] א"כ נסגוד לרוחא דמבדר עננא. א"ל נסגוד לרוחא. א"ל ונסגוד לבר אינש דסביל רוחא. א"ל מילין את משתעי. אני איני משתחוה אלא לאור. הרי אני משליכך בתוכו. ויבא אלוה שאתה משתחוה לו ויצילך הימנו. הוה תמן הרן קאים פליג. אמר מה נפשך אם נצח אברהם אנא אמר מן דאברהם אנא. ואם נצח נמרוד אנא אמר דנמרוד אנא. כיון שירד אברהם לכבשן האש וניצול. אמרין ליה דמאן את. א"ל מן דאברהם אנא. נטלוהו והשליכוהו לאור ונחמרו בני מעיו. ויצא ומת על פני תרח אביו. הה"ד (במדבר יא) וימת הרן על פני תרח וגו': (כ) ויקח אברם ונחור להם נשים וגו'. אברם היה גדול מנחור שנה א'. ונחור היה גדול מהרן שנת א'. נמצא אברהם גדול מהרן שני שנים. שנה לעיבורה של מלכה ושנת לעיבורה של יסכה. הרן מוליד לששה שנים. ואברם אינו מוליד אתמהא: (כא) ותהי שרי עקרה וגו'. אמר ר"ל בכל מקום שנא' אין לה הוה לה. ותהי שרי עקרה אין לה ולד הוה לה. וה' פקד את שרה וגו'. (ש"א א) ויהי לפנינה ילדים ולחנה אין ילדים והוה לה. (שם ב) כי פקד ה' את חנה ותהר ותלד וגו'. (ירמיה ל) ציון היא דורש אין לה. הוה לה. (ישעיה נט) ובא לציון גואל (שם נד) רני עקרה לא ילדה פצחי רנה וצהלי:

סדר לך לך

פרשה לט

(א) **ויאמר** ה' אל אברם לך לך מארצך וגו'. א"ר יצחק פתח (תהלים מה) שמעי בת וראי והטי אזנך ושכחי עמך ובית אביך. א"ר יצחק משל לאחד שהיה עובר ממקום למקום. וראה בירה אחת דולקת. אמר תאמר שהבירה הזו בלא מנהיג. הציץ עליו בעל הבירה. א"ל אני הוא בעל הבירה. כך לפי שהיה אבינו אברהם אומר תאמר שהעולם הזה בלא מנהיג. הציץ עליו הקב"ה וא"ל אני הוא בעל העולם. (שם) ויתאו המלך יפיך כי הוא אדניך. ויתאו המלך יפיך ליפותיך בעולם. והשתחוי לו. הוי ויאמר ה' אל אברם:

יד יוסף [illegible]

מתנות כהונה

[illegible]

ענף יוסף

[illegible]

עץ יוסף

[illegible]

סדר לך לך

פרשה לט

[illegible]

It would seem that the primary transmission of the orally transmitted Torah originally took the form of teachers instructing their students in the law. With time, however, this method could have led to the tradition becoming forgotten, for it depended upon both the quality of the teachers and a stable political and economic atmosphere conducive to study. Indeed, we find that in the period after the death of Moshe, three hundred *halachos* were forgotten and were only reestablished through Osniel ben Knaz's ability to derive them exegetically from the written Torah (see *Temurah* 16a). It was thus imperative that a parallel method be established to ensure the continuity of the orally transmitted Torah. It is this parallel method that we refer to as *Midrash halachah.* While the methodology itself will be discussed in Part IV, note should be taken of the halachic works that have been transmitted to us separately from the Talmud. They include the *Mechilta,* the halachic *midrash* to *Shemos*; *Toras Kohanim,* also known as the *Sifra Dvei Rav*, and the *Sifra,* the halachic *midrashim* to *Vayikra*; and the *Sifri*—the halachic *midrash* to *Bamidbar* and *Devarim*. There is no extant halachic *midrash* to *Bereishis*. These works, which also contain some aggadic materials, were redacted by the schools of the *tanna'im* R. Yishmael ben Elisha and R. Akiva.

The *Midrash aggadah* consists of ethical sayings, parables, and stories, sometimes directly related to a scriptural verse (as is the case with *Midrash Rabbah*) and sometimes a series of aggadic material independent of contiguous scriptural linkage (as is the case with *Pirkei d'Rebbi Eliezer*). There is no certainty as to the date of the final editing of the major *midrashim*. It should be noted that some of the aggadic material quoted in the *Midrash* finds its parallel in the Talmud, although it is not unusual to find details in one that are missing in the other. For example, the Talmud (*Gittin* 57b) relates the story of a woman whose seven sons were killed by Caesar. The *Midrash* (*Eichah Rabbah*) retells the same incident, adding that the woman's name was Miriam bas Nachtom. (Josephus is the source of the similar story about Chana and her seven sons at the time of Antiochus.) Sometimes there are substantive differences between the version quoted in the Talmud and that brought in the *Midrash*. For example, the Talmud (*Gittin* 56a) quotes R. Yochanan rebuking R. Zechariah ben Avkilus for having convinced his colleagues not to kill Bar Kamtza and thus preventing him from reporting back to the emperor. The version brought in the *Midrash* maintains that R. Yochanan chided R. Zechariah for not having rebuked Kamtza when he refused to allow Bar Kamtza to remain in his home.

15.1 *Midrash Rabbah*

Midrash aggadah to the Torah and five *megillos*. The *Midrash Rabbah* is the most widely known of the many *midrashim* and consists of exegetical materials from both the *tanna'im* and *amora'im*. A number of major commentaries are usually found including:

15.1.1 *Yafeh To'ar* and *Yafeh Anaf* Commentaries by R. Shmuel Yaffa Ashkenazi (Turkey—16th century), rabbi in Constantinople. *Yafeh To'ar* is a commentary on *Midrash Rabbah* to the Torah, whereas *Yafeh Anaf* is the commentary to the *Midrash* on the five *megillos*.

15.1.2 *Matnas Kehunah* Commentary by R. Yissachar Berman ha-Kohen (Poland—late 16th to early 17th century). A student of R. Moshe Isserles, R. Yissachar Berman strived to clarify the plain meaning of the text as well as to correct and emend it. His commentary has been printed in almost every edition of *Midrash Rabbah* and is especially valuable in understanding Latin and Arabic terms.

15.1.3 *Chidushei Radal* Commentary by R. Dovid Luria (Lithuania—1798–1855). R. Dovid was one of the rabbinic leaders of his generation and, together with R. Yitzchok of Volozhin, met with Sir Moses Montefiore when the latter traveled to eastern Europe to investigate the condition of the Jews. In addition to his commentary to

Midrash Rabbah (printed in the Romm edition), he wrote a commentary to *Pirkei d'Rebbi Eliezer.*

15.1.4 ***Eitz Yosef* and *Anaf Yosef*** Commentaries by R. Chanoch Zundel ben Yosef (Poland—d. 1867). The work was divided into two sections: *Eitz Yosef,* which provides the simple meaning of the *Midrash,* and *Anaf Yosef,* which is a homiletical exposition on the material. R. Chanoch Zundel also wrote commentaries to the *Tanchuma* with the same titles.

15.1.5 ***Maharzu*** Commentary by R. Zev Wolf Einhorn (Lithuania—19th century), printed in the Romm edition.

15.2 *Pirkei d'Rebbi Eliezer*

Midrash aggadah ascribed to the *tanna* R. Eliezer ben Hyrkanus. Unlike *Midrash Rabbah, Pirkei d'Rebbi Eliezer* does not follow the order of the books of the Torah. Rather, it follows a chronological order beginning from the Creation. R. Dovid Luria (see 15.1.3) wrote a commentary to the work.

15.3 *Pesikta d'Rebbi Kahana*

Midrash aggadah ascribed to the *amora* R. Kahana. The *Pesikta* is arranged according to the portions of the Torah read on festivals, holidays, and the four special *Shabbosos* (i.e., *Shekalim, Zachor, Parah,* and *ha-Chodesh*). The *Pesikta Rabbasi* would seem to be a combination of materials taken from the *Pesikta d'Rebbi Kahana* and the *Tanchuma.*

15.4 *Tanchuma*

Midrash aggadah arranged according to the weekly Torah reading ascribed to the *amora* R. Tanchuma. Though some portions begin with a halachic question prefixed by the phrase *yilamdenu rabbenu*—instruct us teacher—these would seem to have been inserted as a rhetorical means of introducing a discussion rather than as an attempt to find a source for *halachah.* For the most part, the answers to these questions are quite obvious and refer to well-known *halachos.*

15.5 *Yalkut Shimoni*

Midrash aggadah to the entire *Tanach,* compiled by R. Shimon *ha-Darshan* of Frankfurt (Germany—13th century). While much of the material contained in the *Yalkut* can be found in the Talmud and *Midrash Rabbah,* portions of it must have been collated from *midrashim* that are no longer extant.

15.5.1 *Zayis Ra'anan* Explanatory notes to the *Yalkut* by R. Avraham Abeli Gombiner (the *Magen Avraham*—see 11.8).

15.6 Other *Midrashim*

In the commentaries of the *rishonim* and *acharonim,* the student will often find references to other *midrashim.* For the most part, these are collections of homilies and parables drawn from earlier *midrashim,* some of which are no longer extant. It is not unusual to find commentaries quoting materials that do not appear in any of the midrashic literature that has come down to us. The following collections of *midrashim* are often quoted:

Midrash Abba Gurion to *Esther*
Midrash Lekach Tov to the Torah
Midrash Shmuel
Midrash ha-Gadol to the Torah
Midrash Mishle
Midrash Shocher Tov

16

Philosophical and Ethical Literature

The literature of Jewish philosophy and ethics is directly linked to the world of *halachah* and *aggadah,* for our relationship to God, to our fellow man, and to ourselves is part and parcel of the Torah. As the map by which man is to be guided in this world, the Torah provides us with a philosophy of life and a code that ensures ethical behavior. The works of scholars and rabbis who sought to create and provide answers to the questions that troubled their generations are not only based upon the Torah, but are, in reality, works of Torah interpretation themselves. *Halachah* and *aggadah* are not points of departure from which an author develops his own system that might be similar in concept or direction to the Torah. On the contrary, as the eternal message of the Eternal God, *halachah* and *aggadah* have within them the ability to answer and face any and every contemporary challenge. One must simply search within their words to find the why and how of life, for they are eternally relevant.

The following works represent but the tip of the iceberg; they have been chosen because they are representative of the basic source materials that the student will likely come across as he begins his studies.

We have limited ourselves to the works of one of the *geonim* and to the *rishonim;* later works are so numerous that an attempt to be selective would be impossible. The works cited are complex and may be beyond comprehension by the beginner. Nevertheless, in that they are often quoted by other "less difficult" works, we have seen fit to mention them.

16.1 *Emunos ve-Deos*

Philosophical work written by R. Sa'adiah Gaon (b. Egypt—882, d. Bavel—942). R. Sa'adiah was the only non-Babylonian ever to serve as head of one of the two major Babylonian academies, heading the yeshivah in Sura from 928 on. Before coming to Bavel we know that he spent some time in Aleppo, Syria, and it was there that he led the battle against the ruling of R. Aharon ben Meir, head of the yeshivah in Jerusalem, regarding the Jewish calendar. The yeshivos of Eretz Yisrael traditionally set the calendar, and R. Aharon insisted that it was his right, as head of the major academy in Israel, to decide when the festivals would be celebrated. The *geonim* of Bavel, however, felt that his calculations were mistaken and refused to acknowledge his authority.

It should be noted that this disagreement was not merely jurisdictional or theoretical, but had major ramifications. Were Babylonian Jewry to abide by a calendar different than that followed by the Jews of Eretz Yisrael—e.g., by celebrating the festivals at different times—a schism would develop that would undoubtedly lead to the creation of two Judaisms. R. Sa'adiah shared the opinion of the Babylonian *geonim* and strived to convince R. Aharon to accept their calculations but to no avail. R. Sa'adiah wrote a full account of the dispute in his *Sefer ha-Mo'adim*.

R. Sa'adiah was the most vociferous antagonist of the Karaites—the sect begun in the eighth century by Anan ben David—who denied the authenticity of the rabbinic tradition and followed a code based on a literal interpretation of the Torah. (The Hebrew name *Kara'im* is a reference to those who follow the *mikra*—the text.) The *Sefer ha-Kabbalah* of R. Avraham ben Dovid (Spain—1110–1180)—referred to as Ra'avad I to distinguish him from R. Avraham ben Dovid who wrote the *hasagos* to the Rambam's *Yad ha-Chazakah*—notes that Anan broke from tradition when he was not appointed exilarch (political leader of Babylonian Jewry). The sect was consolidated by Binyamin ben Moshe in the ninth century, and he was the first to use the term *Kara'im* (Karaites).

Emunos ve-Deos is the earliest philosophical work that has come down to us. Written in Arabic, it was translated into Hebrew by R. Yehudah Ibn Tibbon (father of R. Shmuel—see 16.4) in 1186. R. Sa'adiah also wrote an Arabic translation of *Tanach* (the first in a language other than Aramaic or Greek), which he called *Tafsir*. Unlike other authors who wrote in Arabic, R. Sa'adiah used the Arabic alphabet rather than Hebrew.

Although many later authors differed with R. Sa'adiah's philosophical views, he was held in the highest esteem and is considered to have provided the impetus for those who followed to engage in and write works of philosophy. The Rambam (*Iggeres Teiman*) writes: "Were it not for R. Sa'adiah, the Torah would have been forgotten by Israel."

16.2 *Chovos ha-Levavos*

Philosophical work by R. Bachya Ibn Paquda (Spain—11th century). R. Bachya (not to be confused with R. Bachya ben Asher, a disciple of the Rashba who wrote a commentary to the Torah) lived in Saragossa. In his work he stresses that the conceptual *mitzvos* (the *chovos ha-levavos*—duties of the heart) are as an important a part of Judaism as are the practical *mitzvos*. Written in Arabic, the work was translated into Hebrew by R. Yehudah Ibn Tibbon at the request of R. Meshullam of Lunel, teacher of the Ra'avad (see 8.1 and 9.1) and R. Zerachiah ha-Levi (see 8.3).

16.3 *Kuzari*

Philosophical work written by R. Yehudah ha-Levi (b. Spain—1075, d. Eretz Yisrael—1140), a disciple of the Rif. R. Yehudah ha-Levi, who supported himself by practicing medicine, also wrote many poems and songs that have become part of our liturgy (e.g., the *kinah* ציון הלא תשאלי and the *zemer* for *Shabbos* יום שבתון). His songs and prose evidence his great longing for Eretz Yisrael, a desire that he fulfilled when he decided to leave Spain and move to Israel despite the dangers involved (it being the years of the Second Crusade). According to legend, he was trampled to death by an Arab horseman when he reached the gates of Jerusalem.

The *Kuzari* was written in the form of a dialogue between a king and a rabbi whom he had summoned to teach him about Judaism and prove its superiority over other religions. Based on the historical conversion of King Bulan of Khazar and his people in the eighth century, the *Kuzari's* dialogue covers the entire spectrum of Jewish belief. Written in Arabic, it was translated into Hebrew by R. Yehudah Ibn Tibbon. The importance of the work as a fundamental exposition of Jewish philosophy is attested to by the words of the Vilna *Gaon* who wrote (*Ma'asei Rav*): "The *Kuzari* is holy and pure and the essentials of Jewish belief are dependent upon it."

16.4 *Moreh Nevuchim*

Philosophical work by the Rambam (see chap. 9), written in Arabic and translated into Hebrew by R. Shmuel Ibn Tibbon at the request of

R.Yehonasan of Lunel in consultation with the Rambam himself. (Although he did not ask R.Shmuel to translate the work—and, indeed, was certainly capable of writing it in Hebrew had he so chosen—the Rambam did correspond with him and answered a number of questions that R.Shmuel posed to him regarding its contents.)

Moreh Nevuchim (Guide for the Perplexed) was written in Egypt, while the Rambam served as court physician to the viceroy. Because of its reliance on Aristotelian philosophy and its rational explanation of miracles, publication of the Hebrew translation of the *Moreh Nevuchim* created a storm of protest in Spain and France. R.Meir ha-Levi Abulafia (Spain—1170–1244—author of the talmudic commenatry *Yad Ramah* and a colleague of R.Avraham ha-Yarchi on the *beis din* of Toledo) wrote a strong protest to the rabbis of Lunel who had arranged for the Rambam's works to be published in Hebrew. He was joined by R. Avraham Min ha-Har (Montpellier) and R.Yonah of Gerona (see next entry) who saw many of the Rambam's statements in the *Moreh* (and in the first section of the *Yad ha-Chazakah*) as heretical. A ban was placed upon reading the work, which was answered by a counterban by the rabbis of Lunel.

An attempt to mediate the dispute was made by the Ramban, but it is difficult to ascertain how successful he was. We do know that copies of the *Moreh Nevuchim* were burned by Dominican monks in Paris in 1242. Indeed, when the destruction of the Rambam's works was soon followed by the burning of twenty-four wagon loads of the Talmud, R.Yonah understood the latter tragedy as a heavenly omen that opposition to the Rambam and his works had gone too far. He publicly recanted and vowed that he would travel to the Rambam's grave to beg his forgiveness.

The controversy flared up again in the beginning of the fourteenth century. The Rashba signed a ban against the study of philosophy before the age of twenty-five, a ban that R.Menachem Meiri opposed.

16.5 *Sha'arei Teshuvah*

Philosophical and ethical work by R. Yonah of Gerona (Spain—1200–1263). A cousin of the Ramban (as well as an in-law, for his daughter married the Ramban's son), R. Yonah was a disciple of R. Avraham Min ha-Har and R. Moshe of Evreux—one of the authors of the Tosafos. He founded a yeshivah in Barcelona and was an active participant in the controversy surrounding the works of the Rambam (see above). R. Shlomo ben Aderes (the Rashba—see 3.2) was his student. On his way to Eretz Yisrael, which he had vowed to visit in order to beg forgiveness at the grave of the Rambam, he visited Toledo, and at the appeal of its citizens agreed to temporarily settle there and establish a yeshivah. He died suddenly in Toledo and was thus unable to fulfill his vow.

IV

DYNAMICS OF TALMUDIC DIALOGUE

One of the fundamental roles of the Talmud is to establish that the halachic system is consistent with the Torah. The Torah does not always deal in specifics nor does it delineate what must be done in every instance. Thus, there must be a means of establishing that a decision reached—or a specific practice—is true to the Torah's intent. Furthermore, while all of *halachah* is part of the *Torah she'ba'al peh*—the orally transmitted tradition handed down from Sinai—the persecutions and exiles to which the Jews were subjected led to a state wherein much of this tradition was in danger of being forgotten. Indeed, it was this very factor that led R. Yehudah *ha-Nasi* to decide that the orally transmitted Torah should be committed to writing. It is thus imperative that a method exist to establish the authenticity of the halachic system.

There are three methods that the Talmud uses to establish a practice as being consistent with the Torah. One, the concept of *halachah le-Moshe mi-Sinai*—a tradition handed down from Moshe—does not require textual support. Its quotation as being the source for a tradition or *halachah* is accepted without requiring further textual or logical support. A prime example of the use of this concept are the laws concerning *tefillin*. Inasmuch as the citation of a practice or law as being obligatory as a *halachah le-Moshe mi-Sinai* is almost always accepted without debate, we have chosen not to discuss it in this work.

The two primary tools that the Talmud employs in establishing the link between accepted practice and the Torah are *drash*—derivation—and *sevara*—logic. The second method is actually preferred. The student will often find the Talmud noting, "Why is the verse necessary, is it not logical?" The upshot of this statement is that the Talmud saw it as axiomatic that the Torah would not speak of something that man can determine on his own. The very fact that the Torah found it necessary to mention a law or obligation indicates that the said law was not obvious in and of itself.

A source for accepted practice that is related to *drash* and that the student will often come across is *asmachta*—linkage. Briefly, *asmachta* is used to establish a textual linkage for a rabbinic—as opposed to a Torah—obligation. The linkage is not strong enough for us to establish the law as being a Torah requirement, but is considered to be a partial basis for the sages' establishment of a *halachah*. It should be noted that the authority of the sages to initiate rabbinic obligations is independent of the existence of an *asmachta*.

17

Rules of Derivation

As a general principle, it is safe to contend that *drash* has two major purposes:

A. As a means of reconstructing the forgotten source of accepted *halachos.*

B. As a means of showing that a halachic practice is consistent with the Torah.

The first formulation of a system of rules through which *halachah* could be derived from the Torah was made by Hillel. His seven rules of derivation (see *Tosefta, Sanhedrin* 7:11) were not his creation. Rather, he formulated existing rules that were a part of the oral tradition. At the time of the destruction of the second *Beis ha-Mikdash,* two other rules of derivation were formulated by R. Nechunyah ben Hakanna and Nachum Ish Gamzo.

R. Yishmael ben Elisha, a disciple of R. Nechunyah ben Hakanna, reformulated the rules of derivation into thirteen principles. His formulation is based on the principle (*Sanhedrin* 64b) "that the Torah uses the language of man," i.e., not every word of the Torah is necessarily open to interpretation and/or deduction, for words or letters might well have been employed for "literary" and stylistic purposes. However, the method with which the Torah expressed laws could be used as a means of reconstructing the *halachah*—e.g., *klal uprat*. In R.Yishmael's view then, the words themselves might not serve as a source for derivation, in that they may serve other purposes, but the form and structure in which they are used can be employed as a means of deduction. His colleague, R.Akiva, contested this view as will be seen.

17.1 The Thirteen Principles of R.Yishmael

R.Yishmael's formulation of the rules of derivation can be subdivided into two categories:

A. ***Midrash Hamekish***—derivations based on comparisons.
B. ***Midrash Hamevaer***—derivations based on textual explanations.

The following are the rules of derivations based on comparisons:

17.1.1 Kal Vachomer An *a fortiori* assumption, i.e., if the known laws applying to X are more stringent than those that apply to Y, then a stringency that applies to Y is surely true of X. The converse of this assumption is also valid. Thus, if X is more stringent than Y, then a leniency that applies to X is surely true of Y.

We find that the Torah itself uses *kal vachomer*. The verse (*Devarim* 31:27) states: *And if when I was alive among you, you rebelled against Hashem, surely after my death* [*you will do so*]. The sages (*Bereishis Rabbah* 92) note ten examples of *kal vachomer* that appear in *Tanach*.

As noted, *kal vachomer* can be used in either direction; i.e., to apply a leniency to Y based on its being true of X, or to apply a stringency to X based on its being true of Y. For example, the restrictions regarding forbidden types of work are more extensive as regards *Shabbos* than as regards the Festivals. Thus, *Shabbos* can be seen as being more stringent than the Festivals. It therefore follows that if a specific type of work is forbidden on the Festivals, it would surely be forbidden on *Shabbos*. Conversely, if a specific type of work is permitted on *Shabbos,* then it would follow that this type of work would surely be permitted on the Festivals.

While it would seem that *kal vachomer* is a purely logical process—and thus should not be included as one of the principles of derivation—it is included as such since its use is predicated on a base whose law is known from the Torah. This base law is then compared to another law, giving us information about the latter.

Because *kal vachomer* is a logical process, it can be used by a sage without him having to first establish that it is based on a received tradition. Hence, another sage can contest its validity by refuting the underlying logic. The use of *kal vachomer* presupposes that all of the relevant *halachos* are known to the person making the *kal vachomer;* otherwise his assumption that the basic law is either more stringent or lenient than the derived law might be mistaken. There are a number of other restrictions that govern the use of *kal vachomer.*

A. ***Dayo Lavo Min Hadin Lihyos Kanadun***—the derived law must be equivalent to the law from which it was derived; i.e., if we apply a law to X based on its being true of Y, the application to X cannot be any more stringent than it is for Y.

For example, the Mishnah (*Bava Kamma* 2:5) discusses the extent of liability X has if his ox causes damage to Y's ox in the latter's domain. The sages maintained that X is liable for half damages—which would be the case if X's ox had damaged Y's in the public domain—whereas R.Tarfon maintained that he must pay full damages.

R.Tarfon argued that the law of damages in the public domain had to be seen as being less stringent than the law of damages done within Y's domain. If X's ox ate or trampled Y's property within the public domain, X would not be liable, whereas he would be liable for full damages if his ox did so in Y's domain. Hence, damages done by X's ox in Y's domain should be seen as being more stringent than damages done in the public domain. Logically then, in a situation where X would be liable for half damages in the public domain—i.e., if his ox gored Y's—he would be even more culpable if that same type of damage was done in Y's domain and should pay full damages.

The sages answered that since the liability of X for the damages his ox had done by goring Y's ox in Y's domain was derived from the known law of goring in the public domain, the extent of his liability in the latter case could be no greater than they are in the former case. The derived law—goring in Y's domain—could be no more stringent than the base law—goring in the public domain. Consequently, just as X was liable for half damages in the public domain, he could only be liable for half damages if the goring took place in Y's domain.

B. *Kal vachomer* is limited to Torah law. Since the basis of many Rabbinic ordinances is the desire to erect a protective fence around the Torah—*seyag* in talmudic terminology—a specific stringency enacted in one case cannot be assumed to be applicable in another case, for the rabbis might not have seen a need to be stringent in the latter situation.

For example, the Mishnah (*Yadayim* 3:2), in discussing levels of ritual impurity, quotes the opinion of R. Yehoshua that when a hand with a second level of ritual impurity comes into contact with the other hand, the latter is considered to have a second level of ritual impurity. The sages maintained that a second level of impurity cannot affect something else. R. Yehoshua argued that we had seen that the sages had elsewhere decreed that something judged to have a second level of ritual impurity could affect an object with which it came into contact. The sages answered that one cannot draw analogies between laws of the Torah and rabbinic decrees nor between one rabbinic decree and another.

C. *Kal vachomer* is not used to draw a comparison from a law based on *halachah le-Moshe mi-Sinai*.

For example, the Talmud (*Nazir* 57a) discusses the question of whether a *nazir* becomes ritually impure if he comes into contact with a *revi'is* of blood. R. Akiva maintained that he would, utilizing a *kal vachomer* analogy. R. Eliezer answered that the *kal vachomer* analogy could not be used. R. Yehoshua explained that R. Akiva's *kal vachomer* could not be used because it was based on a comparison to a law based on a *halachah le-Moshe mi-Sinai*.

D. *Ein Onshin Min Hadin*—*Kal vachomer* cannot be used to establish punishment; i.e., the penalty imposed upon one who violates the original law cannot be assumed to apply to the derived law.

For example, the Talmud (*Sanhedrin* 74a) questions whether one is permitted to kill a person to prevent him from worshiping idols. R. Shimon maintains that one may do so and employs the following *kal vachomer*. If one is permitted to kill a rapist to prevent him from defiling a woman, one is surely permitted to kill an idolator to prevent him from defiling the honor of God. The Talmud rejects this analogy, rhetorically asking, "Can punishment be derived through a *kal vachomer?*"

17.1.2 *Gezerah Shavah* An analogy based on the use of the same term in two separate cases. When the Torah utilizes a specific term in one case and then uses that same term in another case—even though the latter has no logical relationship to the former—we can draw an analogy between the two laws. Use of this principle allows for the creation of an entire halachic system based on a minimum of text.

On the surface, *gezerah shavah* would seem to be completely illogical—as if we were drawing an analogy between the traits of fruits and vegetables. However, if one accepts the axiom that the Torah does not use superfluous words, one can conclude that the repetition of a specific term in another context is an indication that a comparison can be drawn.

There are two types of *gezerah shavah* used in the Talmud:

A. As a means of clarifying the text. For example, the Talmud (*Kiddushin* 2a) discusses the Mishnah's ruling that a woman can be betrothed through money. The basis for money being used as a means of acquisition in this case is derived through a *gezerah shavah*. The Torah (*Bereishis* 23:13) states that when Avraham purchased the burial field from Efron, he said: *I have given the money for the field, take it* [קח] *from me*. In the verse concerning betrothal, the Torah (*Devarim* 22:13) states: *When a man takes* [יקח] *a woman*. The use of the verb "take" in the latter case is compared to its use in the former case; i.e., just as money is effective as a means of taking a field, so too is it effective as a means of taking a wife.

B. As a means of establishing a *halachah* not mentioned in the text. For example, the Talmud (*Shavuot* 47a) rules that the heirs of a *shomer sachar*—a paid watchman—are not obligated to swear that their father had not used the item that he was being paid to guard—a vow that the father would have to make if the item had been accidentally destroyed while in his custodianship. Through use of a *gezerah shavah,* it is determined that this ruling applies to the heirs of a *shomer chinam*—an unpaid watchman as well, for the Torah (*Shemos* 22:7 and 22:10) uses the phrase *that he has not used his neighbor's property* regarding both the paid and unpaid watchmen. Once the law freeing the heirs of the unpaid watchman has been derived from the Torah, it can be applied to the heirs of the unpaid watchman based on the use of the same phrase.

Gezerah shavah has a number of restrictions that govern its usage.

A. ***Mufnah***—open; i.e., no deductions or inferences were made from the words being compared. The redundancy of the words is taken as an indication that they were utilized to point to the comparison drawn. For example, the Talmud (*Shabbos* 64a) draws a comparison between the laws of ritual impurity of a corpse to those of an insect, noting that the comparison is possible because the similar terminology is open.

B. *Ein Adam Dan Gezerah Shavah L'atzmo*—no one can draw a *gezerah shavah* comparison on his own; i.e., there must be a received tradition that a comparison had been drawn between the two laws. The Rambam (*Sefer Hamitzvos, Shoresh* II) explains this restriction: "The principle of *gezerah shavah* is an instrument that could be used *ad infinitum* to refute all of the laws of the Torah."

If *gezerah shavah* had no restrictions on its use, anyone could freely associate between unrelated subjects and use the repetition of terminology as a means of supporting his contentions. The Talmud therefore rules that *gezerah shavah* can only be used as a means of establishing textual proof for a known tradition and only if the sages had a tradition that a comparison was to be drawn based on the use of similar terminology in two different cases.

C. **Both words or phrases used in the *gezerah shavah* must be from the Torah.** Comparisons cannot be drawn based on the repetition of a term in *Nevi'im* or *Kesuvim*. For example, the Talmud (*Bava Kamma* 2b) questions the source of the Mishnah's ruling that an ox's goring with his horn is a major category of damage. Initially, the Talmud establishes that the source is a verse from *Nevi'im,* but then points out that the latter cannot serve as a source for the Torah.

D. *Ein Gezerah Shavah Lemachtzah*—a partial comparison cannot be drawn; if a law applicable to X is applied to Y through use of a *gezerah shavah,* then all of the laws applicable to X must be applied to Y. For example, the Talmud (*Zevachim* 48a) determines that the sages' decision not to require a guilt offering of a person whose use of consecrated property was doubtful was based on the fact that a *gezerah shavah* comparison had been drawn between the sin offering and the guilt offering in a different context. Thus, since the latter was not applicable in cases of doubt, the former would also not be applicable in cases of doubt.

There are two other methods of derivation often used in the Talmud that are not considered to be separate principles, but rather subcategories of *gezerah shavah,* since their logical basis is similar.

A. ***Hekesh***—juxtaposition of cases, i.e., where a number of cases are mentioned in either a single verse or in a group of verses. Through *hekesh* we can deduce that the law specified in one case applies to the juxtaposed cases as well. For example, the Torah (*Devarim* 22:26) states, in reference to a betrothed woman who was raped: *nothing shall be done to the girl [i.e., she is not to be punished], for she is not liable for the death penalty [as would be the case had she—as a betrothed woman—consented to the act], for just as when a man rises up to kill his neighbor, so too is this case.* The Talmud (*Sanhedrin* 74a) uses the juxtaposition of rape and murder in the verse as the basis for the ruling that one is permitted to kill in self-defense.

The difference between *hekesh* and *gezerah shavah* is that the former is a comparison drawn by the Torah itself, whereas the latter is a comparison drawn by the sages. It is thus understandable why *hekesh* is a preferred means of derivation.

B. ***Semuchim***—juxtaposition of subjects, i.e., a comparison drawn on the basis of the proximity of two subjects. *Semuchim* differs from *hekesh* in that the Torah does not draw a specific analogy, but seems to point to one. For example, the Torah (*Shemos* 22:17) states: *You shall not allow a witch to live.* The next verse states: *Anyone who has intercourse with an animal shall be put to death.* The Talmud (*Berachos* 21b) deduces from the juxtaposition of the two subjects that just as bestiality is a capital crime, so too is witchcraft. R. Yehudah maintains, however, that *semuchim* can only be used as a means of deriving *halachah* if the verses are from *Devarim.*

17.1.3 *Binyan Av* A conclusion drawn from a biblical verse, also referred to as *mah matzinu*—what have we found. *Binyan Av* has two forms; *mikasuv echad,* a conclusion drawn from a single verse, and *mishnei kesuvim,* a conclusion drawn from two verses. For example, the Torah (*Devarim* 19:15) states: *A lone witness shall not testify against a man . . . according to two witnesses or three witnesses the matter shall be established.* The Talmud (*Sotah* 2a) notes that the use of the word witness already indicates that the testimony of a single *witness* is unacceptable; the word *lone* would thus seem to be superfluous. The Talmud concludes that the use of lone as a qualification for the singular *witness* in this verse comes to teach us that if the word witness is used elsewhere without the qualifying *lone,* the reference is to more than one witness even though the singular form is used.

Similarly, the Torah (*Devarim* 23:25–26) states: *If you [i.e., a laborer] come into your neighbor's vineyard, you may eat grapes until you are satisfied but you may not place them into your vessel [for later consumption]. If you [i.e., a laborer] come into your neighbor's standing grain, you may pick sheaves by hand but you may not use a scythe to cut your neighbor's standing grain [for your personal use].* The Talmud (*Bava Metzia* 87b) poses the following question. What is the source of the Mishnah's ruling allowing a laborer to eat produce while working in his employer's field? The first verse cannot be seen as being the source, for one could say that a laborer is permitted to eat the fruits of the vine since in any event the owner is required to leave a portion of that produce for the poor. The second verse can also not be seen as being the source since in any event the owner is required to set aside a portion of that produce as *challah*—one of the twenty-four gifts given to a *kohen*. However, by comparing the common denominator of the two verses, the Talmud concludes that a laborer is permitted to eat everything that grows.

Binyan Av has one restriction; it is only applicable if both of the verses are required to establish the *halachah*. If the second verse simply repeats a law that was already known, no conclusions can be drawn.

The following are the rules of derivations based on textual explanations:

17.1.4 *Klal Uprat* A general category followed by a specific example. Do we say that the specific example is given so as to limit the application of the general category, or do we say that the specific example is no more than an illustration of that application? For example, the Torah (*Vayikra* 1:2) states: *If any of you shall offer a sacrifice to Hashem, you shall bring your sacrifice from animals, from the herd or from the flock you shall offer your sacrifices*. The *Toras Kohanim* (ad loc.) rules that since the word animals is a general category, whereas the words herd and flock are specific examples, all sacrifices must meet the criteria of the specific examples.

The Principle: When a general category is offered followed by a specific example, we rule that the latter serves as a qualification of the former.

17.1.5 *Prat Uklal* A specific example followed by a general category. Again, do we say that the specific example is given so as to limit the law of the general category, or do we say that the specific example is an illustration of the general category's practical application? For example, the Torah (*Devarim* 22:1 and 3) states: *You shall not watch your brother's ox or sheep wandering and ignore them, you shall return them to your brother. You shall do so for his donkey, and you shall do so for his garment and you shall do so for all things which your brother has lost. . . .*

Because the general category—*all things*—follows the specific examples, we rule that the obligation to return lost property applies to all losses and not only to those specified in the verse. The Talmud (*Bava Metzia* 27a) explains that the specific examples cited in the verse teach us various *halachos* regarding the identifying signs and are not superfluous. However, they are not to be understood as limiting the obligation to return lost property in any way.

The Principle: When a general category is preceded by a specific example, we rule that the latter does not serve as a qualification of the former.

17.1.6 *Klal Uprat Uklal* A general category followed by specific examples followed by a general category. Again, we are faced with the same dilemma; do we see the specific examples as limiting the scope of application of the general categories that precede and follow them? For example, the Torah (*Shemos* 22:6–8) states:

> *If a man gives his friend money or utensils to watch and they are stolen from the man's [i.e., the watchman's] home; if the thief is caught, he [the thief] shall pay double. And if the thief is not caught, then the householder [i.e., the watchman from whose house the items were taken] shall come to the court [and swear] that he has not used his neighbor's property. In any case of crime [i.e., in any situation where the watchman claims that the property is no longer in his possession] be it an ox, a donkey, sheep, a garment or any [property that was] lost [and about which the watchman claims that he was not negligent in guarding the property], and about which [testimony is brought] saying this is it [i.e., the property which the watchman claims is no longer in his possession], their claims shall be brought to the court, and he who the court finds culpable shall pay double to his friend.*

In the last verse, the Torah—referring to a case where the owner of the property claims that the watchman was negligent or that he had himself stolen the property—requires the watchman to swear to the court to substantiate his claim. The verse begins with a general category—*in any case of crime*—followed by specific examples—*an ox, a donkey, sheep, a garment*—and concludes with a general category—*any [property that was] lost*. Based on the principles of R. Yishmael, the Talmud (*Bava Kamma* 63a) rules that the law is not limited to the specific examples cited. However, the law is conditional in that it only applies to items that are similar to the specific examples cited. In this case, the Talmud (*Shavuos* 42b) rules that the law that requires the watchman to swear that he was not negligent applies only to items that are similar to an ox, a donkey, sheep, or garments; i.e., that are movable and that have intrinsic value.

The Principle: When specific examples are preceded and followed by general categories, we rule that the application of the law is limited to items that are similar to the specific examples.

17.1.7 *Klal Shehu Tzarich Laprat* A general category that is elucidated by a specific example. The converse of this principle also applies, i.e., a specific example followed by a general rule that serves to elucidate it.

This principle differs from *klal uprat* and *prat uklal* (17.1.4 and 17.1.5) in that here we are dealing with a situation where both the example and the general rule explain each other rather than limiting or expanding a given law. Whereas *klal uprat* and *prat uklal* each contain enough information to enable us to determine the *halachah* and can thus be seen to serve as limiting or expanding the halachic application, *klal shehu tzarich laprat* deals with a situation wherein the specific example and the general rule each provide necessary information for deriving the halachic application. It should be noted that the rules of derivation are used as a means of establishing a source for known halachic practice and are not used as a means of creating new *halachos*.

For example, the Torah (*Shemos* 13:2) states: *Sanctify all firstborn to Me, the issue of all wombs among the children of Israel, among man or beasts, they are Mine*. This *halachah* is repeated later (*Devarim* 15:19) where the Torah states: *Every firstborn that is born among your male herds and flocks shall be sanctified to Hashem*.

The Talmud (*Bechoros* 19a) offers the following explanation. Had we interpreted these verses according to the rule of *klal uprat,* we would see the latter verse's statement of *among your male herds* as qualifying the general rule and limiting its application to males alone. However, had we done so, we would rule that firstborn males would have to be sanctified even if they were preceded by a female. This would contradict the statement of the first verse that had limited the *halachah*'s application to *the issue of all wombs,* which had specifically limited the application to a firstborn whose birth had not been preceded by another birth from that womb.

Moreover, if we limited the *halachah* to those cases that fit the criterion of *the issue of all wombs,* then a male born after a previous cesarean birth would also be included in the obligation since the latter could not be seen as being *the issue of all wombs.* However, the verse in *Devarim* would seem to limit the *halachah*'s application to those who fit the criterion *of all firstborn.* A male born after a cesarean birth would not meet that criterion.

We are thus faced with a situation where the *klal* does not expand the *prat,* nor does the *prat* limit the *klal.* Taken individually, we cannot determine the source for the known *halachah* that the obligation to sanctify the firstborn applies to a firstborn male whose birth was not preceded by another birth—neither of a female nor of a cesarean section. Only when we combine them are we provided with all the information necessary to reach the conclusion.

The Principle: When the *klal* and *prat* serve to explain each other, we combine them so as to derive the *halachah.*

17.1.8 ***Kol Davar Shehayah Baklal Veyatza Min Haklal Lelamed*** An example whose specific applications were already included within the general category. In this case, we are referring to a case wherein the specific example cited by the Torah does not limit the application of the general category, for whatever information that we are provided with by the specific example was already known. Thus, the example cannot be seen as limiting the application of the general category.

Rather, we must see the Torah's citation of what would be an otherwise superfluous example as coming to teach us something completely new that will further elucidate the application of the general category.

For example, the verse (*Shemos* 20:10) states: *and the seventh day shall be* Shabbos *for you, you shall not perform any type of work*. Later, the Torah (*Shemos* 35:3) states: *You may not light fires in all your encampments on the* Shabbos *day*. The latter verse is a specific example of a forbidden type of work. Yet, the lighting of a fire had already been included in the prohibition of the former verse. It cannot be seen as a *prat* following a *klal,* thereby limiting the forbidden type of work mentioned in the first verse, for to do so it would have had to be mentioned within the context of the first verse. Its citation would thus seem to be superfluous unless it had been said to teach us something entirely new.

The Talmud (*Shabbos* 70a) explains that the specific example cited teaches us that each type of work forbidden on *Shabbos* is prohibited individually. Thus, if I perform a single action that is made up of two or more forbidden types of work, I am held culpable for each one, even though I only performed one action. For example, if I light a fire under a pot, I am culpable for both lighting a fire on *Shabbos* and for cooking on *Shabbos*.

The Principle: When a specific example already included within a general category is cited, the specific example comes to teach us something that applies to the entire general category.

17.1.9 *Kol Davar Shehayah Baklal Veyatza Lit'on To'an Echad Shehu K'inyono, Yatza Lehakel Ve-lo Lehachmir* If a specific example was already included within a general category, and it is then cited in a context similar to the general category.

For example, the Torah (*Shemos* 21:12) states: *One who strikes a man causing him to die shall surely be put to death*. No differentiation is made between intentional and unintentional killing. Later, the Torah (*De-*

varim 19:5) states: *and if one came across his neighbor as he cut wood in the forest, and he swung the ax to cut the tree and the head [of the ax] was detached from the handle and fell on his neighbor killing him, he shall flee to one of the cities [of refuge] and remain alive.*

The *Sifri* (ad loc.) explains that the second verse teaches us that unintentional killing is not a capital crime. This rule is then applied to the general category cited in the first verse and qualifies it, limiting the punishment for killing to cases where it was committed intentionally.

The principle differs from *klal uprat* in that the specific example only teaches us something about the general category through inference. Had the second verse specifically stated that only one who kills intentionally is to be killed, we might well have seen its citation as being a *klal uprat*. However, by telling us that a person who kills unintentionally remains alive, we can infer that the punishment cited in the first verse only applies to one who kills intentionally. Thus, it is not really a limitation of the general category cited earlier but a clarification. As such, we rule that the purpose of its being brought in this manner is to teach us to be lenient rather than stringent.

The Principle: When a specific example clarifies details of a general category, we rule leniently and not stringently.

17.1.10 ***Kol Davar Shehayah Baklal Veyatza Lit'on To'an Acher Shehu Lo K'inyono, Yatza Lehakel Ulehachmir*** If a specific example was already included within a general category, and is then cited in a context that is not similar to the general category.

For example, the Torah (*Vayikra* 13:1–3), in discussing the laws of *tzara'as,* rules that a person suffering from the affliction is declared to be ritually impure if a *kohen* discovers a white hair on the afflicted flesh. Later, in discussing *tzara'as* found on the head under the hair or beard, the Torah (*Vayikra* 13:30) seems to limit the application to a case where the hair found was yellow. Thus, though the specific example would seem to limit ritual impurity to cases where a yellow hair was found—as would be true were we to employ the rule of *klal uprat*—we cannot do so since this specific example concerns *tzara'as* found under the hair or beard and is thus different than the *tzara'as* found on the flesh that was spoken about earlier. The *Sifra* explains that we therefore take its citation by the Torah as having both lenient and stringent ramifications. Hence, a white hair does not impart ritual impurity if found under the hair or beard, and a yellow hair does not impart ritual impurity if found on the flesh. The yellow hair cited in the specific example thus has stringent applications vis-à-vis *tzara'as* under the hair and lenient applications vis-à-vis *tzara'as* found on the flesh.

The Principle: A specific example that is cited in a context that is not similar to the general category has both lenient and stringent applications.

17.1.11 *Kol Davar Shehayah Baklal Veyatza Lidon B'davar Chadash, I Atah Yachol Lehachaziroh Laklal, Ad Sheyachazirenu Hakasuv Leklalo B'ferush* If a specific example was already included within a general category, and is then cited specifically to teach us something that was not included within the general category.

This principle differs from the previously cited one. The previous principle deals with a situation wherein the information included in the specific example contradicted the information available in the general category. This principle deals with a situation wherein the specific information in the example comes to inform us of an entirely new *halachah*.

For example, the Torah (*Vayikra* 14:13) states: *and he shall slaughter the lamb [offered by the person afflicted with* tzara'as*] in the same place as the sin-offering and burnt-offering are slaughtered in the Sanctuary, for the sin-offering is like the guilt offering, both are the kohen's....* The next verse states: *and the* kohen *shall take the blood of the guilt-offering [brought by the person afflicted with* tzara'as*] and the* kohen *shall place it on the lobe of the* *right ear of the person being purified, and on the thumb of his right hand and on the big toe of his right foot.*

The *Toras Kohanim* (ad loc.) explains that the guilt-offering of *tzara'as* had been a part of the general category of sin-offerings as evidenced by the first phrase of the first verse. The Torah had separated it from the general category by teaching us a specific law applicable only to it, i.e., that the *kohen* was required to take the blood of the offering and place it on the person's ear, big finger, and big toe. Had the Torah not specifically returned the guilt-offering to the general category—in the last phrase of the first verse—we would rule that the laws applicable to the general category would no longer be applicable to it.

The Principle: If a specific example was removed from the general category, the laws applicable to the general category cannot be applied to it unless the verse specifically returns it to the general category.

17.1.12 ***Davar Halamed Meinyano Vedavar Halamed Misofo*** Inferences deduced from the context and inferences deduced from subsequent text.

For example, the Torah (*Shemos* 20:13) states: *You shall not steal.* The text does not specify whether this prohibition applies only to the theft of objects or includes kidnapping as well. The Talmud (*Sanhedrin* 86a) determines that the inclusion of stealing within the context of *You shall not murder* and *You shall not commit adultery*—both of which are capital crimes—can allow us to infer that the prohibition also pertains to kidnapping, which is specified elsewhere to be a capital crime.

Similarly, the Torah (*Vayikra* 14:34) states: *I have put the affliction of* tzara'as *on a house in the land you possess.* The verse does not specify what constitutes a house. A subsequent verse (*Vayikra* 14:45) states: *and the* kohen *shall tear down the house, the stones, the timbers and all of the mortar.* The *Sifra* rules that the latter verse teaches us that the house considered to be afflicted by *tzara'as* is one that was constructed from stones, timber, and mortar.

The Principle: A category can be clarified by its context or by subsequent detail.

17.1.13 ***Shnei Kesuvim Hamakchishim Zeh Es Zeh, Ad Sheyavo Hakasuv Hashlishi Veyachria Beineihem*** Two verses that seem to contradict each other. This principle applies to a situation wherein two verses that deal with the same subject seem to infer contradictory applications. There is no difference whether the two verses appear within the same chapter or in separate chapters. No inference is made until a third verse sheds light on the apparent contradiction.

For example, one verse (*Bereishis* 1:1) states: *In the beginning* Hashem *created the heaven and the earth.* Later, the Torah states (*Bereishis* 2:4): *on the day that* Hashem *created earth and heaven.* The inference from the first verse is that heaven was created first, whereas the inference from the second verse is that the earth was created first. We must therefore turn to a third verse that clarifies the point; i.e., the verse (*Yeshayah* 48:13) that states: *My hand has laid the foundations of the earth and My right hand has spanned out the heaven, I call to them and they come forward together.* Rashi (ad loc.) explains that the creation of the world can be compared to a craftsman who works with both hands simultaneously. Thus, God created the heaven and the earth at the same time and there is therefore no contradiction.

The Principle: When two verses seem to contradict each other, we make no inferences until a third verse resolves the contradiction.

17.2 The Principles of R. Akiva

As we have already noted, R. Akiva did not accept R. Yishmael's basic contention that the Torah used the language of man, i.e., that phrases or words in the Torah might have been used for stylistic rather than deductive purposes. His basic premise in deriving *halachah* from the text was that the language of the text cannot be seen as form; rather every sentence, word, letter, and even crown had been chosen to infer a specific teaching. Thus, many of R. Yishmael's principles of derivation would be inapplicable according to R. Akiva, for instead of seeing the sources as being superfluous phrases used to either expand or limit the law, he would search for the new law to be derived from their very mention.

R. Akiva, in his textual derivations, employed the following two basic principles:

17.2.1 ***Ribui Umiut*** Extension and limitation. Although somewhat similar to R. Yishmael's principle of *klal uprat, ribui umiut* differs in that it places the emphasis on the language employed rather than on the subject matter. According to this principle, words such as אף—*even*, גם—*also*, כל—*all*, and את—a participle used as an introduction for a direct object, extend the *halachah* derived from a specific text. On the other hand, words such as אך—*however*, רק—*only*, and מן—*from*, serve to limit the application of a *halachah* derived from a text.

17.2.2 ***Yesh Em Lamikra*** The manner in which words are pronounced is used to establish *halachah*. Whereas R. Yishmael's principles are based on the manner in which the words of the Torah are transcribed, R. Akiva saw the traditional pronunciation as being the determining factor. It should be noted that there are instances in the Torah of קרי וכתיב—where a word is written one way and pronounced another way. This can have halachic ramifications.

For example, the Talmud (*Sanhedrin* 4a) notes that the Torah (*Vayikra* 12:5) states: *And if she shall bear a girl, she shall be ritually impure* שבעים. Were we to base the *halachah* on the way the word is written, we would render the woman ritually impure for seventy days, for that would be the translation of שבעים. However, according to the way the word is traditionally pronounced, with a *shuruk* under the ב and a *patach* under the ע, the translation is two weeks.

R. Akiva and his students had an enormous influence on the development of *halachah*, for most of the sages of the Talmud followed his methodology. The Talmud (*Sanhedrin* 86a) notes: The author of an anonymous mishnah is R. Meir, an anonymous *tosefta* is R. Nechemyah, an anonymous *sifra* is R. Yehudah, an anonymous *sifri* is R. Shimon—and they all taught according to R. Akiva.

17.3 Additional Methods of Derivation

Aside from the specific principles formulated by R. Yishmael and R. Akiva, we find many other examples of the Talmud using textual analysis as a means of deriving *halachah*. It is beyond the scope of this work to attempt to analyze every form of textual analysis; the following are offered as examples.

17.3.1 Literal versus Nonliteral Interpretation For example, the Mishnah (*Berachos* 1:3) records a dispute between the schools of Shammai and Hillel regarding the obligation to recite the *Shema*. The verse (*Devarim* 6:7) states: *and you shall speak of them when you stay in your house and when you travel on the road and when you lay down and when you arise*. The school of Shammai interpreted the verse literally and ruled that at night the *Shema* must be recited while laying down and in the morning it must be recited while standing. The school of Hillel maintained that the latter phrases are to be understood as teaching us that the obligation is to recite the *Shema* at the time when people are laying down and at the time when people arise.

17.3.2 *Midrash Hahigayon* Derivations based on logical analysis of the text. This differs from the use of *sevara*—logic, which is the topic of the next section, in that it is based on an examination of the text rather than on intuitive deduction.

For example, the Torah (*Devarim* 24:6) states: *you shall not take the lower or upper millstone as a security, for it is his [the debtor's] livelihood.* The Mishnah (*Bava Metzia* 9:13) interpreted this to mean that one may not take any item as surety if it is used to prepare food, for the Torah had stressed that the lender—by taking the millstone as security—would be depriving the debtor from earning a means of livelihood. Thus, it is logical—based on the text's explanation—to expand the *halachah* that the Torah stated to similar articles given as surety for a loan.

Midrash hahigayon is also used to limit the application of a *halachah*. For example, the Torah (*Devarim* 23:4–5) states: *an Amoni and Moavi shall not enter the assembly of Hashem . . . for they did not come forward to you with bread and water when you were on your way out of Egypt.* The Talmud (*Yevamos* 77a) derives that the prohibition of marrying either an Amoni or a Moavi applies only to males. Since the Torah had explained the reason for the prohibition—*because they did not come forward with bread and water*—we can logically conclude that the prohibition applies only to those who would normally provide bread and water; i.e., men and not women.

The sages also used logical interpretation when the text suggested it be employed. For example, the Torah (*Shemos* 12:6) states: *and the entire congregation of Israel shall slaughter it [i.e., the Paschal sacrifice]*. The Talmud (*Kiddushin* 41b) asks: Is it possible for the entire congregation to slaughter the Paschal sacrifice? Surely one person slaughtered it on behalf of the others. Rather, we can logically deduce that the Torah used the phrase *and the entire congregation* to teach us that an action performed by an agent is considered to have been performed by the one who appointed him. Since the slaughterer acted as an agent on behalf of the congregation, it is considered as if the entire congregation had slaughtered the Paschal sacrifice. Logically, then, any action performed by an agent can be considered to have been performed by the person who appointed the agent.

18

Talmudic Logic

As noted, much of the discussion in the Talmud is concerned with reconstructing the exegesis of the Torah. Whereas R. Yishmael and R. Akiva had formulated principles through which this could be accomplished, we find that the Talmud prefers to do so logically whenever possible; i.e., if a law or ruling can be established through logical methods—*sevara* in talmudic terminology—there is no need to revert to exegesis of the Torah. Moreover, the very fact that a law or ruling can be established through logical means is itself indication that the Torah is informing us of a different law or rule; there would be no need to write something that can be understood as being logically imperative.

One type of logical deduction that is quite common in the Talmud is analogy. Because the Torah and its laws are the work of a single source, a principle that applies, for example, to a religious issue can be used to determine a law in a civil issue. Even though the two questions would seem to be unrelated, since they are both parts of the Torah, they are deemed to be analogous and inferences can be drawn between them.

A brief example: The Mishnah (*Bava Kamma* 23b) discusses the question as to when an ox that has gored is considered to be prone to goring—a *mu'ad* in talmudic terminology. The owner of a *mu'ad* is liable for full damages, and the ox must be destroyed. The Torah states (*Shemos* 21:29) *and if it [the ox] is a goring ox from the day before yesterday,* but does not provide us with specific details. R. Yehudah maintains that the ox is classified as a *mu'ad* if it gores over a period of three consecutive days and draws support for his view from an analysis of the redundancies in the text of the verse cited. R. Meir maintains that the ox is classified as being a *mu'ad* once it gores three times, irrespective of whether it does so in one day or over three days. His opinion is based on logic; if an ox that gores over a period of three days is considered to be a *mu'ad,* an ox that gores three times in one day should surely be considered to be prone to goring.

The Talmud questions the validity of R. Meir's logic by noting that as regards the law of *zavah*—a woman who had an emission from her body that renders her ritually impure—she would only enter that state if the emissions were over a period of three separate days. If she had three emissions on a single day, she would not become a *zavah.* Thus, we see that the Torah differentiates between events that occur over a set period of time and between an event that occurs repeatedly within that time framework. By analogy, we could well say that the status of the ox would also be dependent upon the goring taking place over a set period of time rather than within the time framework. Hence, R. Meir's contention that since an ox is considered to be a *mu'ad* if it gored over three days, it is surely a *mu'ad* if it gored three times in a single day, might well be logical but would still be invalid in the face of the evidence drawn from the case of the *zavah.*

Generally, the Talmud's use of *sevara*—logic—can be subdivided into the following categories.

18.1 Common Sense

The Talmud (*Sanhedrin* 74a) poses the following question: What is the source of the known law that rules that if someone tells a person, "kill person X or you will be killed," that he must allow himself to be killed? The Talmud answers that it is a *sevara,* and cites an incident where a person came to Raba and said, "The ruler of the city told me that I must kill a certain person or I will be killed." Raba told him, "You must allow yourself to be killed for who is to say that your blood is redder than his." Rashi comments that no man has the right to decide that his life is more valuable than another's. Thus, we see that the Talmud uses common sense to establish a law whose application is of no minor significance.

The Talmud (*Kesubos* 22a) rules that if a woman testified that she had previously been married but had received a proper divorce, she is believed without having to bring corroborating proof; e.g., her bill of divorce. Since we only know that she was married—and thus theoretically unable to marry someone else—through her testimony, her claim to have received a proper divorce is also accepted without her having to substantiate it. In talmudic terms, this type of logic is referred to as *ha'peh she'asar hu ha'peh she'hitir*—the testimony that prohibited—i.e., the woman's admission that she had previously been married—is the testimony that permits—i.e., the woman's claim that she had received a proper divorce. Common sense dictates that if we accept her original testimony as being valid without substantiation, we should also accept her later testimony as being valid without need for corroboration. This type of logic is closely related to *miggo,* discussed in section 18.5.

18.2 *Chazakah*—Conclusions Based on Observation

Because the Torah was given to man so that he might live according to its imperatives, *halachah* must be consistent with the manner in which people usually act or react. By observing normative occurrences and behavior, and basing their rulings to specific questions accordingly, the sages of the Talmud could be assured that their legislation was consistent with the Torah's spirit and thus halachically appropriate. One of the most common forms of observation found in the Talmud is *chazakah*—presumption. *Chazakah* can be divided into a number of subcategories:

18.2.1 Status Quo We presume that a situation is unchanged until evidence is presented substantiating the change. For example, what would happen if a man appointed an agent to deliver a bill of divorce to his wife in a different city? The agent's ability to act on behalf of the husband is contingent upon the husband being alive when the divorce is actually delivered. Were he to die in the interim, the agency would be cancelled and the divorce document would be meaningless. The Talmud (*Gittin* 28a) rules that a man who was known to be alive is presumed to still be alive. Thus, we presume that just as the man was alive when he appointed the agent, he is still alive when the agent delivers the divorce.

Similarly, we presume that a physical condition remains unchanged until we have evidence of such change. For example, the Talmud (*Bava Basra* 153b) rules that in the case of a terminally ill person, an oral declaration is sufficient to transfer title to property and the usual means of acquisition need not be employed. What would happen if two parties contested ownership of property, X contending that the former owner had orally transferred title to him when he was terminally ill, and Y contending that the former owner was well at that time and that the oral transfer was therefore invalid? *Chazakah* enables us to presume that the previous owner's present physical state was true of him when he made the oral transfer, i.e., if he is terminally ill now we can presume that he was terminally ill at the time that he made the oral transfer. Conversely, if the previous owner is well now, we can presume that he was also well at the time of the oral transfer.

The familiar talmudic concept of *ha'motzi mechavero alav lehavi ra'ayah* is based on *chazakah*—status quo, i.e., if X claims that Y owes him money or that the object in Y's possession is his, the burden of proof is on X, for we assume that whoever has possession of an object is its owner unless proof is offered to substantiate the claim.

18.2.2 Specific Types of Behavior Behavior can also be used as the basis for logical presumption. For example, the Talmud (*Kiddushin* 80a) rules that we can establish the existence of a forbidden relationship based on our observation of behavior. Thus, if evidence was presented that a woman had engaged in sexual relations with a child, the fact that the child was observed clinging to the woman would be sufficient to establish that the woman was the child's mother and that the relationship was thus incestuous.

18.2.3 Normative Behavior The behavior of most people in a given situation can also be used a means of establishing a logical presumption. For example, if X claims that Y owes him money, and Y claims that he has repaid the debt, the burden of proof is on X even though Y admits that there was such a debt. The Talmud (*Bava Metzia* 3a) bases this ruling on the logical presumption that man is not brazen to his creditors, i.e., he would not have the audacity to lie to a man who had given him a loan. He is therefore presumed to be telling the truth until such time as his creditor can prove that he is lying.

Conversely, we can employ the normative behavior of people to establish that a debt remains unpaid. For example, if X claims that Y had promised to repay a loan at a specific time, Y's claim that he repaid the loan earlier than promised is not believed. The Talmud (*Bava Basra* 5a) explains that people do not repay loans before they are due. Thus, the burden of proof would be placed on Y, for he would have to substantiate that he had acted in departure from normative behavior.

Another example of normative behavior used as a means of establishing logical presumption is the statement of R. Yitzchak that people are in the habit of constantly checking their pockets. The application will be explained in the analysis of a talmudic discussion in chapter 20.

18.2.4 Repeated Occurrences If a situation occurs a number of consecutive times, we presume that it will continue to occur unless proved otherwise. For example, if a woman's child dies as a result of circumcision, and her subsequent child also dies as a result of circumcision, the Talmud (*Yevamos* 64b) rules that we do not circumcise her subsequent children for we presume that they too will die as a result of circumcision. It should be noted that this type of presumption is usually made only after an event has occurred three consecutive times.

18.3 *Bereirah*—Retroactive Decisions

Another method of talmudic logic is *bereirah*—choice; i.e., retroactively applying a definition that only became clear later to resolve a matter that was in doubt. The use of *bereirah* would allow us to define the past by granting retroactive powers to the present; i.e., we would be able to make a halachic ruling by declaring *a posteriori* that the lack of information that caused our doubts to arise in the first place is no longer an impediment once we have defined the terms or objects that caused those doubts to arise.

For example, the Mishnah (*Gittin* 3:1) poses the following question: Is it halachically appropriate for a man to tell a scribe to write a bill of divorce for one of his wives without specifying which wife he wants to divorce? Can we say that the husband's later decision to use the bill of divorce for one of his wives is a retroactive indication that he had intended to divorce that specific wife when he told the scribe to write? The Mishnah rules that the bill of divorce is invalid since the Torah requires that a bill of divorce be written for the purpose of divorcing a specific woman. Since no specific woman had been specified when the bill was written, it would be invalid. However, had there been no such requirement, *bereirah* could well have been used as a means of determining the husband's intent.

Similarly, the Talmud (*Gittin* 47a-b) poses the following question. A

Jew and non-Jew own a field in partnership, and the produce of the field has not been tithed or had *terumah* (the portion of the produce given to a *kohen*) separated. Can we say—through *bereirah*—that when the non-Jew takes his portion of the produce, this retroactively indicates that the remaining produce belonged to the Jew and is the portion that must be tithed?

Bereirah could also be used to retroactively validate an act to which a condition had been applied. For example, if a man says to a woman that their betrothal should be affected through cohabition on the condition that her father agrees, can we say that if the father does not agree, this retroactively invalidates the act of coition as a means of betrothal, even though it had been performed to establish the woman as his wife? It should be noted that the Talmud questions whether *bereirah* would apply in this situation since the determination is not in the hands of the person who made the stipulation.

18.4 *Rov*—A Majority of Cases

An additional method of talmudic logic is based on the results of a majority—*rov* in talmudic terminology. Similar in concept to *chazakah,* it is essentially a means of presumption based on statistical analysis. *Rov* presumes that what is true about a majority of cases is true of a specific case as well. While *rov* would seem to be a more definitive means of making a presumption, its dependence on numbers makes it less definite when the minority is substantial. Nevertheless, the Talmud (*Niddah* 18b) rules that when *rov* contraindicates *chazakah, rov* is followed.

Two types of *rov* are used in the Talmud.

18.4.1 A Majority That Is Observable We can assume that a specific item shares the same properties as the majority of similar items. For example, if there are ten butcher shops in a specific area, nine of which stock kosher meat and one of which stocks nonkosher meat, we can presume—based on *rov*—that a piece of meat found in the street came from one of the kosher butcher shops. The talmudic expression used to describe this majority is *kol d'paresh mirubah parush*—that which was separated, was separated from the majority. It applies to people as well as to objects.

18.4.2 A Majority That Is Not Observable At times, the Talmud will presume something to be true even though there is no means of statistically determining it to be true. Our observation of human behavior can lead us to make a presumption that the majority of people act in a certain manner or that what is true of most people is true of a specific person as well. For example, since most men are not impotent, we can assume that a couple has had a sexual relationship (see *Yevamos* 13:12).

Presumptions drawn on the basis of *rov* can be negated by the halachic principle of *kavua*—fixed. Although the explanation we offer is simplistic, this latter principle can be seen as an either/or dilemma. Previously we noted that if one found meat in the street, one could presume that the meat was kosher if the majority of butchers in the area stocked kosher meat. However, what happens if a person purchased meat and could not remember if he had purchased it from the kosher butcher or from the nonkosher butcher. In the previous case, the person who discovered the meat never knew its original status. We could therefore presume—based on the majority—that its source was the kosher butcher. In the latter case, the status of the meat was once known—it was *kavua* or fixed. The person who forgot is faced by a dilemma that has an either/or resolution; i.e., he either purchased it from a kosher or a nonkosher butcher. He therefore cannot rely on the majority of stores to presume which was the source of the meat.

The question of when to follow *rov* and when to declare something as *kavua* has been the subject of halachic discussions for hundreds of years. Generally, we can state that *kavua* takes precedence over *rov* in a situation where one was once aware of the status of the subject in question.

18.5 *Miggo*

In establishing the credibility of a person's testimony, the Talmud often employs the concept of *miggo*. *Miggo*—loosely translatable as "since"—enables us to draw a conclusion based on a presumption that the end result could have been accomplished in a different manner. A *miggo* lends credence to a plea that would otherwise have to be substantiated by establishing that we should believe what is being said since the person could have said something else that would have been believed and would have brought about the same result.

For example, the Talmud (*Bava Basra* 50b) discusses the Mishnah's ruling that a husband's use of his wife's property cannot be seen to be evidence that the property is his, even though similar usage would normally be sufficient means to establish property rights. Consequently, the woman need not declare that her husband's use of the property is not to be taken as indicating that she has relinquished title. This declaration—*macha'ah* in talmudic terminology—is usually required to retain one's rights when another person has use of the property. What would happen if another person—let's refer to him as X—used the property, claiming that he had purchased it from the husband who had purchased it from her? We would expect that the burden of proof would be on X, since the woman is not required to declare that her husband's use of her property should not be taken as indication that she has relinquished her rights to it. The Talmud rules, however, that because we would believe X if he claimed that he had purchased the property directly from her—since there had been no declaration during the period when he had used the property—X's claim that he had purchased the property from the husband is credible.

The Shach (*Choshen Mishpat,* end of 82) defines *miggo* in the following manner:

> He is presumed to be telling the truth, for had he wished to tell a lie, a better plea—i.e., one which the court would have accepted—would have been open to him.

Rav Herzog (Main Institutions of Jewish Law I) further clarifies the concept:

> If X makes a statement which does not appear probable on the face of it, this fact will not tend to weaken his case if he could have made another statement which would have appeared probable. If that other statement would have been acceptable to the court, the one that he actually makes must also be accepted, for had he wished to tell an untruth, he would have made that other statement.

The limitation on the use of *miggo* in substantiating claims is the subject of extensive discussion in the Talmud and commentaries, and there are many conditions attached to its use.

It should be noted that *miggo* is sometimes used as a form of analogy. For example, the Talmud (*Sukkah* 7a), notes that since two full walls and a third wall of a *tefach* are considered to be the three walls necessary for a *sukkah,* they are also considered to be three walls to render an area a private domain vis-à-vis the laws of *Shabbos*.

19

The Structure of Talmudic Dialogue

As a means of familiarizing the student with the methodology and style of talmudic discussion, and to give the reader a "taste" of the contributions made by the commentators towards our understanding of the discussion, we shall offer an example drawn from the second chapter of *Bava Metzia* (folios 21b through 22b).

A number of points should be clarified before we begin. The Talmud's discussion of a question is often based on a statement of the Mishnah. Whereas the Mishnah informs us of a law pertaining to a specific case, the discussion in the Talmud often proceeds to examine how that law can be applied in other cases. At times, the Talmud seeks to determine the underlying principle of the law so that it can be applied to cases that are slightly different from the example cited in the Mishnah. Some discussions concern themselves with finding support for a law cited in the Mishnah—either through scriptural exegesis or logic. Proof and rebuttal are offered from a variety of sources and their introduction sometimes leads the discussion to digression from the subject of the Mishnah. At other times, the quotation from a *tanna* or *amora* leads the Talmud to quote additional citations from that sage even if they are not pertinent to the subject being discussed.

The example to be offered concerns the law of found property. The Torah (*Devarim* 22:1) states clearly that one is required to return lost property. Obviously, if one saw property being dropped and can immediately return the lost property to the owner, one must do so. Failure to return the property would render the finder a thief, for the property would be considered to have come into his possession illegally. The Torah's requirement obligating one to return lost property must therefore be seen as also applying to a case where one finds property and does not know who lost it.

The Mishnah clarifies this law by explaining that it applies to properties that have an identifying sign, i.e., a means through which the owner can establish that the found property is his. The Mishnah rules that a person finding property that has an identifying sign must announce his discovery so that the owner will have the opportunity to prove that it is his. The owner's familiarity with the identifying sign is taken as proof that the property found is his. We assume that were it not his, he would be unaware of the identifying information.

The Mishnah also rules that the discovery of some types of found property need not be announced since the lack of an identifying sign precludes the possibility of the owner offering proof that they are his.

For example, the Mishnah notes that if one finds money spread out on the street—the fact that it is spread out indicating that it was lost rather than placed there purposely—one need not announce the discovery since money has no unique identifying sign. However, if one found the money in a wallet, the discovery would have to be announced since the wallet is itself a unique identifying sign that the owner could provide to indicate that the found property is his.

Rashi explains the reason why one need not announce the discovery of something that has no identifying sign. We assume that the owner—knowing that he has no means of establishing that the loss is his—gives up hope of recovery, and the property is therefore considered to be ownerless. Rashi's introduction of the seemingly unrelated concept of the property being ownerless bears further examination.

What makes something the property of a person? According to *halachah,* something becomes mine when I acquire it through a valid means of acquisition—a *kinyan.* The type of *kinyan* employed depends upon the nature of the item being acquired. Thus, some properties are acquired by lifting them while others are acquired by pulling or pushing them. If the property is ownerless, it becomes mine when I perform the requisite act of *kinyan.* However, if the property belongs to someone else, the act of *kinyan* alone cannot make the item mine. The agreement of the previous owner to relinquish his claim in favor of someone else is necessary before my act of acquisition can be effective. This agreement is referred to as *da'as makneh* in talmudic terminology.

In the case of found property, the agreement of the previous owner to relinquish his title to the property is lacking. How then can the item become the property of the person who found it? Rashi therefore notes that if the previous owner gives up hope of recovery—*yiush*—the property is considered to be ownerless—*hefker* in talmudic terms. The finder can therefore acquire title by simply making a *kinyan.*

However, if the found property had an identifying sign, the owner would not give up hope of recovering the lost item. Therefore, the *kinyan* of the finder would be ineffective since the previous owner had not relinquished his title and the finder is not acquiring property that is ownerless. The finder, were he to take the property as his own, would be a thief, for he would be appropriating property belonging to someone else.

The Talmud then proceeds to raise an interesting point. What happens if the owner is unaware of the fact that he has lost an article that has no identifying sign? Do we say that the article is considered to be ownerless since the person who lost it will give up hope once he discovers that it has been lost? Or, do we say that since he is still unaware of his loss, the property remains his until such time as he discovers the loss and actually gives up hope of recovery?

This question was the subject of a dispute between Abbaye and Rava. Abbaye maintained that the item does not become ownerless until such time as the owner discovers its loss and actually gives up hope of recovery. Rava maintained that the item is considered ownerless even before the owner discovers his loss. Since there is no identifying sign, we can assume that the owner will give up hope when he discovers his loss. Consequently, the item can be considered ownerless from the moment it is found.

The *Ra'avad* raises the following question. The subject debated by Abbaye and Rava would seem to be related to the issue of whether a later clarification can be seen as applying retroactively. This issue, *berairah*—choice—in talmudic terminology, is the subject of discussions in many different tractates and has been explained in 18.3. There are many halachic ramifications to this question that are beyond the scope of this work, but as a means of understanding the scrutiny to which *halachah* is subjected, it is of interest to us.

The *Ra'avad* questions why our discussion should not be seen as being an extension of this debate. Abbaye would seem to maintain that a clarification has no retroactive application while Rava would seem to maintain that it does.

The *Or Somayach* (R. Meir Simcha of Dvinsk, 1843–1926) answers that the discussion in our text is unrelated to the question of whether a clarification has retroactive application. That discussion is dependent upon whether one sees an event taking place or a decision being made as being able to resolve an earlier question. Our discussion is concerned with the question of whether a lack of knowledge can be seen as preventing an item from becoming ownerless. Even were Abbaye to agree that information can be seen to have a retroactive effect, he would still maintain that the lack of knowledge at the time when the item was found precluded it from becoming ownerless and the finder thus must be seen as having acquired it in a prohibited manner. Other commentaries offer other explanations to explain the differences between the two discussions. Again, we present this question as an example of the type of scrutiny to which all talmudic debates are subject in the commentaries. *Halachah* must be consistent, and rulings in one case must be applicable in all similar situations or they are invalid.

Let us now see how the Talmud discusses and resolves the question. Our explanation of the Talmud's discussion is based upon Rashi's commentary unless otherwise noted.

20

An Analysis of a Talmudic Discussion

איתמר, יאוש שלא מדעת—The question was raised concerning a found item that the owner does not know he has lost, but that we assume he will give up hope of recovering when he becomes aware of his loss.

אביי אמר לא הוי יאוש, ורבא אמר הוי יאוש—Abbaye said this is not considered to be giving up hope, i.e., the original owner cannot be considered to have relinquished his ownership, thereby allowing the finder to acquire the item. Rava said this is considered to be giving up hope, i.e., although the original owner is still unaware of his loss, since he will undoubtedly give up hope of recovery once he discovers that the item is no longer in his possession, the item is considered to be ownerless once it is lost and the finder can therefore acquire it.

בדבר שיש בו סימן כולי עלמא לא פליגי דלא הוי יאוש—If the lost item has an identifying sign, all agree that there is no giving up of hope if the owner is unaware of his loss. The finder cannot acquire title to the item before the owner becomes aware of the loss since the previous title has not been relinquished and the item is not considered to be ownerless.

ואף על גב דשמעיניה דמיאש לבסוף לא הוי יאוש—Even if we hear that the owner gives up hope when he discovers his loss—e.g., if he says woe is to me for I have lost the item—the property is not considered to already have been ownerless when found; i.e., we do not apply his expressed *yiush* retroactively.

כי אתא לידיה באיסורא הוא דאתא לידיה—For when the item came into the possession of the finder, it was still the property of the owner. Note that the Talmud uses the term איסורא—prohibited. Because the lost item has an identifying sign, normative behavior leads us to presume that the owner has not given up hope of recovery and has therefore not relinquished his title. The finder is duty bound to return the lost object—by announcing his discovery so that the owner can provide the identifying sign and reclaim it—and if he fails to do so, and keeps the object for himself, he is a thief.

דלכי ידע דנפל מיניה, לא מיאש—Since the item has an identifying sign that the owner can use to prove that the property is his, when he discovers his loss he will not give up hope of recovering it.

Tosafos notes that even though we hear him give up hope of recovering the lost property, this is considered to be circumstance and cannot be considered to have rendered the property ownerless at the time that it was lost. *Halachah* is based on normative behavior. The fact that the owner gives up hope of recovery when he discovers his loss has no retroactive effect since most people would not give up hope of recovering a lost item that has an identifying sign.

מימר אמר סימנא אית לי בגויה, יהבנא סימניה ושקילנא ליה—He will say to himself, when he discovers his loss, I have a means of identifying the property as mine. I will offer my identifying sign and reclaim it.

Note that the Talmud's discussion is based on the assumption that the original owner will act in what can be considered to be the normal fashion. This assumption is itself based on the Mishnah that ruled that the discovery of items that lack identifying signs need not be announced since we assume that the owner has given up hope of recovery.

Having established that the question can only concern an item that has no identifying mark, the Talmud now proceeds to further limit the scope of the disagreement between Abbaye and Rava.

בזוטו של ים ובשלוליתו של נהר, אף על גב דאית ביה סימן רחמנא שרייה— If the item was lost to the tides of the sea or in the currents of a river, then the item becomes the property of the finder even though the item has an identifying sign and even though the owner is still unaware of his loss.

The Torah ruled that this type of loss immediately renders an item ownerless. Since the circumstances surrounding the loss would normally preclude its being returned, the fact that the item has an identifying sign would not lead the owner to retain hope that it will be recovered and returned. Abbaye would also agree that in this situation the property becomes ownerless upon loss even though the owner has not yet indicated that he has given up hope of recovery.

כדבעי למימר לקמן—As we shall see further on, i.e., as the Talmud will prove from a scriptural citation that will be quoted later in the discussion.

כי פליגי בדבר שאין בו סימן—The disagreement between Abbaye and Rava concerns an item that has no identifying sign.

אביי אמר לא הוי יאוש, דהא לא ידע דנפל מיניה—Abbaye contends that the owner cannot be considered to have given up hope of recovery since he is still unaware of his loss. Thus, the item cannot be considered to be that of the finder since it is still owned by the previous owner and the former's act of acquisition is meaningless since title has not been relinquished.

רבא אמר הוי יאוש, דלכי ידע דנפל מיניה מיאש—Rava contends that the owner is considered to have given up hope from the time of the loss and not from the time when he discovers his loss. Since we can logically assume that he will give up hope when he discovers the loss since the lost item has no identifying sign, the property is considered to be ownerless immediately and the finder can thus acquire it.

The Talmud explained that Abbaye held that the property cannot be considered ownerless if the owner is unaware of his loss. Even though we can assume that he will give up hope of recovery once he discovers that he has lost an item that has no identifying signs, until such time as he indicates that he has given up hope, he will not have relinquished his title and the finder can therefore not acquire it. Thus, according to Abbaye, the expression of giving up hope is a necessary precondition to the property becoming ownerless and thus acquirable by the finder.

Why then would Abbaye agree that if the tides washed away an object, the item is deemed ownerless even if the owner has not yet given up hope of recovery? The Rashba points out that even if the original owner specifically states that he has not given up hope of recovering the item, it is still considered to be ownerless once it is washed away.

The answer is that the Torah itself rendered the item ownerless. Just as the Torah has the authority to make something the property of someone, so too does it have the authority to render something ownerless and thus acquirable. Whereas in other situations Abbaye maintains that the decision is contingent upon the will of the owner, this specific situation—in which hope for recovery is obviously impossible—is considered equivalent to the loss of an item that the owner has given up hope of recovering. The owner's unwillingness to give up hope is ignored in the face of normative behavior.

Rava, on the other hand, did not view the actual giving up of hope as a precondition for rendering something ownerless. The loss itself rendered the item acquirable by the finder. However, this acquirability would be limited by the owner's failure to give up hope of recovery. If the owner had no such hope—even if he failed to express this because he was unaware of his loss—the item can be considered to be ownerless and thus acquirable by the finder.

Having established the basis for the divergent opinions of Abbaye and Rava, the Talmud proceeds to establish which viewpoint is halachically correct by offering proofs from various other sources that deal with similar questions. This system of proof and rebuttal is representative of talmudic dialogue, for the opinion of an *amora* has to be consistent with other statements cited in the Mishnah or *beraisa.*

The text of our editions states סימן: פמג"ש ממקטג"י ככסע"ז in parentheses. This is a mnemonic device, each letter representing the first word of one of the sources cited to resolve the dispute.

תא שמע פירות מפוזרין, הא לא ידע דנפל מידיה?—Come and hear, i.e., our Mishnah itself would seem to offer a resolution to the question, for it states that if one finds fruit spread out on the street, one need not announce the discovery. The Mishnah would seem to be referring to a case where the owner was unaware of the fact that the fruits had been lost, yet the Mishnah rules that they become the property of the finder. This would seem to pose a problem for Abbaye, for according to his opinion, the fruits should not be acquirable by the finder until the owner becomes aware of his loss and gives up hope of recovery.

הא אמר רב עוקבא בר חמא הכא במכנשתא דבי דרי עסקינן—Abbaye answers that the Mishnah poses no difficulty, for R. Ukva bar Chama had already explained that the case cited in the Mishnah was referring to the time when the produce is gathered.

דאבידה מדעת היא.—This is considered to be a loss of which the owner is aware, i.e., produce found in the street is considered to have been abandoned and therefore becomes the property of the finder.

תא שמע, מעות מפוזרות, הרי אלו שלו. אמאי הא לא ידע דנפל מיניה?—Come and hear that the Mishnah seems to pose another problem for Abbaye, for it states that money found spread out in the street is the property of the finder even though the owner is not aware of his loss.

Thus, it would seem that the Mishnah is of the opinion that since he will give up hope of recovery once he becomes aware of his loss—since the money has no identifying sign—the finder can acquire the money even before the owner gives up hope.

התם נמי כדרבי יצחק, דאמר אדם עשוי למשמש בכיסו כל שעה—There too the reason is as explained by R.Yitzchak who said, in a different connection, that people are in the habit of constantly checking their pockets, i.e., no inference can be drawn from the Mishnah's ruling, for the case of money found scattered in the street differs from the question under discussion.

In the case of the Mishnah, we can assume that the owner is already aware of his loss before the finder discovers the money. Consequently, the finder is deemed to have found ownerless property and can thus acquire it. R.Yitzchak's description of normative behavior—though cited in another context—is offered by Abbaye as proof that the reason why the money is deemed ownerless is independent of the question as to whether a finder can acquire property before the owner has given up hope of its recovery.

הכא נמי, אדם עשוי למשמש בכיסו בכל שעה ושעה—Here too; i.e., in the case of our Mishnah, the reason why the money is the property of the finder is because people are in the habit of constantly checking their pockets. This clarification resolves the question posed from the Mishnah. Here again we see where normative behavior forms the basis for *halachah.*

תא שמע, עיגולי דבילה וככרות של נחתום הרי אלו שלו. והא לא ידע דנפל מיניה?—Come and hear, i.e., the Mishnah would seem to present another case that can resolve the dispute, for it rules that strings of figs and baker's bread belong to the finder even though the loser has not yet discovered his loss. Again, this would seem to support Rava's contention that property that has no identifying sign is acquirable even before the original owner has given up hope of recovery.

התם נמי אגב דיקירי מידע ידע בהו.—There too; i.e., in the case cited, since they are valuable, we assume that the owner is immediately aware of the loss and has already given up hope of recovery before the finder took possession.

The *Gra* notes that according to the text of the *Rosh,* the word חשיבי—significant or important—should be substituted for the word יקירי. Because foodstuffs are important, we can assume that the original owner continuously checks to see whether he still has them in his possession. Consequently, it is unlikely that he would be unaware of their loss.

The *Beis Yosef,* in his commentary to the *Tur,* offers the following explanation to justify the original text and the emendation of the text by the *Rosh*. The *Rosh* understood the word יקירי as meaning heavy; he therefore emended the text to read חשיבי—important—since the former term was obviously not applicable to figs and bread. However, if one understands the word יקירי as meaning valuable, the text need not be changed.

The *Gra,* in his glosses, also raises a question. The Mishnah had ruled that the discovery of bundles of grain in the public domain need not be announced, mentioning them before strings of figs or baker's bread. Yet, the Talmud does not cite this ruling as posing a difficulty to Abbaye's opinion even though the same question could be asked, i.e., why are they the property of the finder if the owner is not yet aware of their loss?

He explains that the Talmud did not do so because it had already been determined that the Mishnah was referring to bundles of grain that had been purposely put down, for one does not drop a bundle of grain without realizing that one has done so. The reason why their discovery need not be announced is because they are considered to have been willfully abandoned—as seen by the fact that they were left in the public domain. Thus, this ruling has no bearing on the subject under discussion and is therefore not raised as a question to Abbaye's opinion.

Note that the Talmud, in resolving the apparent difficulty that the Mishnah's ruling poses to Abbaye's opinion, uses the phrase התם נמי—there too. The significance of this phrase is that the Talmud is making a comparison to the principle that had earlier been quoted in the name of R. Yitzchak. Although R. Yitzchak had only stated that people are in the habit of checking their pockets regarding money, by logical extension one can make the same assumption regarding anything of value or of importance. The phrase התם נמי would thus imply that even though we find no one specifically stating this principle regarding items other than money, logic dictates that it is true of important or valuable property as well.

תא שמע, ולשונות של ארגמן הרי אלו שלו. ואמאי הא לא ידע דנפל מיניה?—Come and hear, the Mishnah said that if one finds tongues of purple wool, they belong to the finder and their discovery need not be announced. Again, this would seem to pose a problem to Abbaye for the owner is not aware of his loss.

התם נמי, כיון דחשיבי משמושי ממשמש בהו.—There too; i.e., in the case of tongues of purple wool cited in the Mishnah, since they are important, the owner continuously touches them to see if they are still in his possession. Consequently, we can assume that he was aware of his loss before the finder discovered them and he had already given up hope of recovering them, thus rendering them ownerless and acquirable. Again we find the Talmud relying upon the logical principle that is the basis of the statement of R. Yitzchak.

The citation that tongues of wool need not be announced and belong to the finder would seem to be redundant, especially in view of the fact that the Talmud resolves the difficulty posed to Abbaye in the same fashion as it had resolved the previous question. The Ramban explains that the Talmud was not sure whether they too would be considered important; i.e., would we apply the logic of R. Yitzchak that people are in the habit of continuously checking whether an item is still in his possession in this case as well. The fact that the same logical principle was applied thus serves to extend its application.

The Ritva notes that the Talmud does not pose questions to Abbaye from the Mishnah's rulings that strings of fish or pieces of meat belong to the finder even though the owner is unaware of their loss. He explains that since these cases are identical to those already cited, they would be explained in the same fashion; i.e., because they are important, the owner is in the habit of checking that they are still in his possession and we can assume that he had given up hope of recovery before they were found. Posing them as questions to Abbaye would thus be redundant.

Having established that the rulings of the Mishnah are consistent with Abbaye's contention, the Talmud now turns to other sources, examining whether they too are not problematic. Note again that the Talmud does not resolve the questions by simply concluding that Abbaye or Rava disagreed with these sources. As *amora'im,* Abbaye or Rava could not do so unless the sources cited were themselves the subject of disagreement between *tanna'im.* The fact that the sources are quoted anonymously is taken as indication that they represent accepted rulings, and as such, both Abbaye and Rava must prove that their opinions are consistent with these sources.

תא שמע, המוציא מעות בבתי כנסיות ובבתי מדרשות ובכל מקום שהרבים מצויין שם, הרי אלו שלו—Come and hear, if one finds money in the synagogues, or in the study halls, or in any place frequented by the public, they are his, i.e., the finder need not announce his discovery.

מפני שהבעלים מתיאשין מהם—Because the owner gives up hope of their recovery. As Rashi had explained earlier, if the owner gives up hope of recovery, the property is considered to be ownerless and the finder can acquire it.

והא לא ידע דנפל מיניה?—But the owner does not realize that he has dropped them? Again, this would seem to pose a problem to Abbaye who had said that the property was not ownerless until such time as the owner actually discovered his loss.

אמר רבי יצחק, אדם עשוי למשמש בכיסו בכל שעה.—R.Yitzchak explained, people are in the habit of constantly checking their pockets. Since most people behave in a certain manner, we can assume that this person also acted in this manner and is already aware of his loss and has given up hope of recovery when the finder discovered the money. This *beraisa* is the source of R.Yitzchak's statement that the Talmud had quoted previously to resolve the questions posed to Abbaye from the Mishnah.

Tosafos raises two interesting questions. One, why does the Talmud pose a question from the *beraisa* regarding money that was found when it had already posed and resolved a similar question from the Mishnah? Second, why did R.Yitzchak only offer his description of normative behavior as an explanation for the *beraisa*'s ruling when he could have done so to explain the Mishnah?

Tosafos answers that the Talmud had thought that the case of the *beraisa* was stronger proof than the ruling of the Mishnah, for the former would seem to maintain that the discovery of the money need not be announced even if it had an identifying sign since it had been found in a public place. Moreover, the case of the *beraisa* would seem to be referring to a situation where the original owner was still in the synagogue or study hall. Nevertheless, based on R.Yitzchak's description of normative behavior, we assume that the owner is immediately aware of his loss. Thus, the ruling of the *beraisa* is an expansion of the ruling of the Mishnah, for in the case cited in the Mishnah we might assume that the owner only gives up hope of recovery afterward, whereas the *beraisa*'s ruling allows us to assume that he gives up hope of recovery immediately.

The Talmud, having found that Abbaye's opinion was consistent with the rulings of the Mishnah and *beraisa* on the laws of discovered property, now poses a question from a Mishnah in tractate *Pe'ah*.

תא שמע, מאימתי כל אדם מותרים בלקט—Come and hear, from when may anyone take *leket* (the portion of produce that must be left ungathered in the field for the poor to take).

Leket is the property of the poor, i.e., it is left specifically for the poor and may not be gathered by others. Should one who is not poor go into the fields and gather the left grain, he would be considered to have stolen the produce, for the original owner is deemed to have transferred his rights to the produce to those who fit the halachic qualification of being poor. Because of this understood condition, the *leket* is considered to be the property of the poor. However, if the poor had gone into the field and had themselves left some of the grain behind, we can assume that the poor had relinquished their claim to the grain and it would therefore become ownerless and thus acquirable by anyone. The Mishnah therefore seeks to establish when the grain is considered to be ownerless.

משילכו בה הנמושות. ואמרינן מאי נמושות? ואמר רבי יוחנן סבי דאזלי אתיגרא. ריש לקיש אמר לקוטי בתר לקוטי.—From the time when the stragglers have gone through the field, the remaining grain can be considered to be ownerless and anyone can go into the field and collect it. The Talmud, before proceeding to note the problem that this Mishnah seems to pose to Abbaye, first seeks to establish a precise definition for stragglers. R.Yochanan said that the reference is to the old men who need assistance while walking. Since they take their time when going through the fields, we can assume that no one will follow them and any grain left behind is ownerless. Resh Lakish said that the reference is to those who follow the initial group of gatherers; once they have gathered whatever the first group left behind, we can assume that no one else will bother to look for leftover produce in the field. Consequently, anything left behind can be considered ownerless and may be taken by anyone.

ואמאי? נהי דעניים דהכא מיאשי, איכא עניים בדוכתא אחריתי דלא מייאשי? —Why is this so, i.e., why do we consider the grain ownerless and acquirable once the stragglers have gone through the field? Albeit, the local poor can be considered to have abandoned their rights to the produce, for once the stragglers have gone through the field they will assume that there is nothing left for them to take. However, there are poor in other places who have not yet abandoned their rights. The latter are not yet aware that the field has been visited by the stragglers. Consequently, they may still think that there is produce left in the field and may intend to go and gather it. Thus, how can we rule that the remaining produce is considered to be ownerless and thus free for anyone to take? It would seem that the reason is that since they will learn that the stragglers had already been in the field, they will then decide that there is no point in going there to look for grain. Thus, though they still are unaware of this fact, it is as if they already had relinquished their rights to the produce.

The Mishnah's ruling would thus seem to be problematic for Abbaye, for it would seem to support Rava's contention that property can be considered ownerless even before the owner has given up hope. In this case, the poor from other cities are not yet aware that the stragglers have gone through the field. Nevertheless, we rule that once the stragglers have in fact done so, the remaining grain is free for anyone to take. This would seem to prove that Rava's opinion was correct.

Note that the Talmud poses a question to Abbaye from a source that is not referring to lost property, but rather to abandoned property. Abbaye could not contend that he had only ruled that property was deemed ownerless once the original owner had actually relinquished his rights in cases of property that had been lost. This contention would be logically untenable, for what basis would there be to differentiate between lost property and property that had been abandoned by the poor? If property that is abandoned—even unknowingly as in the case of *leket*—is considered to be ownerless, then property that the owner has lost and will certainly give up hope of recovering should also be considered ownerless.

אמרי, כיון דאיכא עניים הכא, הנך מעיקרא איאושי מיאשי, ואמרי עניים דהתם מלקטי ליה.—We say, since there are poor people here (i.e., in the locality of the field) the poor from other places have given up hope (i.e., relinquished their rights to the *leket*) from the beginning, for they will say that the poor there—in the locality of the field—will take the *leket*.

Abbaye answers that the Mishnah's ruling concerning *leket* poses no problem. The basis for allowing anyone to take produce once the stragglers have left the field is independent of the question being debated. The reason why the produce is considered ownerless is because the poor in other cities had never had any hopes of being able to gather *leket*. They would assume that the local poor would take everything from the field. Thus, they had never really had any claim to the produce. We therefore need not wait for them to relinquish their claim based on the fact that the stragglers had entered the field before we allow anyone to take the remaining produce.

תא שמע, קציעות בדרך, ואפילו בצד שדה קציעות,—Come and hear, figs that had been cut from the tree and placed on the road so as to allow their juices to flow out, and even if the figs are found next to a field full of figs laid out to dry. Rashi notes that the Mishnah's ruling applies even if one knows that the figs on the road are part of those left to dry in the field.

וכן תאנה הנוטה לדרך ומצא תאנים תחתיה—And similarly, a fig tree that hung over the road and one found figs underneath, i.e., on the road and not in the field.

מותרות משום גזל ופטורות מן המעשר.—They are permitted and one who takes them is not considered to have stolen them and they need not be tithed. The fact that they are found in the road makes them ownerless, and as such, they may be taken and need not be tithed since ownerless property is not bound by that obligation.

בזיתים ובחרובים אסור.—As concerns olives and carobs, however, they are forbidden, i.e., they may not be taken.

This Mishnah would seem to be problematic to both Abbaye and Rava. The ruling would seem to be based on the premise that since they had been found on the road, the owner could be assumed to have abandoned his claim to them. On the surface, it would further seem that this ruling is true whether or not the owner was aware of their being on the road. The ruling concerning figs would seem to contradict Abbaye—for according to his opinion they should not be ownerless until such time as the owner had actually given up his claim. The ruling concerning olives and carobs would seem to contradict Rava—for according to his opinion they too should be deemed ownerless immediately.

רישא לאביי לא קשיא. אגב דחשיבי ממשמש בהו.—The first statement—i.e., the ruling concerning figs—is not problematic for Abbaye. Since they are valuable, he—the owner—continuously checks them. Hence, we can assume that he is aware of their loss even before they were found and has already given up hope of recovery. Again, the Talmud utilizes the previously cited statement of R. Yitzchak as the basis for a specific ruling.

תאנה נמי מידע ידיע דנתרא.—As regards the ruling concerning figs found under a tree hanging over the road, he—the owner—is aware that some are destined to fall, i.e., the owner is considered to have already relinquished his rights to the figs that eventually fall even while they are still on the tree. Hence, the Mishnah's ruling is again independent of the subject under debate, for it does not refer to a situation wherein the owner gave up hope of recovery after the finder had discovered the property.

Tosafos explains that since the owner knows full well that some figs will fall from the tree onto the road, he abandons his claim to the ones that fall even before they do so. We assume that he says to himself that people walking on the road will take the figs that fall, assuming that they had been dropped by someone walking on the road. As in the case of R. Yitzchak, normative behavior establishes the law. As concerns olives and carobs, however, we make no such assumption since they do not usually fall from the tree. The owner will eventually abandon hope of recovery. However, since he has no reason to assume that some have fallen, we cannot consider them ownerless until such time as he is actually aware of the fact that they have fallen onto the road.

אלא סיפא לרבא קשיא, דקתני בזיתים ובחרובים אסור.—The latter ruling of the Mishnah is problematic for Rava, for it states that olives and carobs are prohibited, i.e., they are not considered to be ownerless even though we can assume that the owner will abandon hope of recovery once he discovers that they have fallen off the tree onto the road. According to Rava's opinion, they should be ownerless once they have fallen even if the owner is unaware.

אמר רבי אבהו, שאני זית הואיל וחזותו מוכיח עליו—R. Avahu explained that the case of olives (and carobs) is different, for their appearance indicates where they are from.

ואע"ג דנתרין זיתי, מידע ידיע דוכתא דאינש איניש הוא.—Even when they fall off the tree, everyone knows that olives found near a tree came from that tree. Rashi explains that we cannot assume that the owner will give up hope once he learns that the olives (or carobs) have fallen from the tree. He will assume that they are still recoverable since people are aware that olives found near a tree most likely have fallen from that tree, and they will return them to him. Thus, according to Rava, the olives and carobs cannot be considered ownerless even though they were found on the road, for we have reason to assume that the owner will not give up hope of recovery.

אי הכי, אפילו רישא נמי?—If this is true, the same should apply to the Mishnah's first statement. If we accept R. Avahu's contention that the owner will not give up hope of recovery because he assumes that the property is still recoverable, why did we rule that figs may be taken? Why did we not rule that they are prohibited because those who find them will assume that they fell from the tree hanging over the road and the owner can therefore not be presumed to have given up hope even though he knows that some will fall?

אמר רב פפא, תאנה עם נפילתה נמאסת.—Rav Pappa answered, the case of figs is different, for when a fig falls from the tree, it becomes squashed.

Rashi explains that figs are deemed ownerless—even according to Abbaye—for two interdependent reasons:

A. **The owner knows that figs are bound to fall from the tree.** However, this in itself would be insufficient grounds for us to assume that the owner has already given up hope of recovery, for we could say that the owner will assume that the person finding them will return them since it is obvious from where they have fallen.

B. **R. Pappa therefore added that when figs fall off the tree, they become squashed.** Hence, the owner can be considered to have rendered those destined to fall *hefker,* for he has no desire to recover squashed figs. Consequently, figs found on the road may be taken, for the owner has already relinquished his claim to them.

תא שמע, הגנב שנטל מזה ונתן לזה, וכן גזלן שנטל מזה ונתן לזה, וכן ירדן שנטל מזה ונתן לזה, מה שנטל נטל, ומה שנתן נתן—Come and hear, a thief (i.e., one who steals without the owner being aware of the theft) who took something from one party and gave it to another, and a robber (whom the owner saw stealing his property) who took something from one party and gave it to another, or the river Jordan that took something from one person and gave it to another; what has been taken is taken and what has been given is given; i.e., the property becomes that of the person who received it.

בשלמא גזלן וירדן, דקא חזי להו ומיאש—It is understandable as concerns the robber and the Jordan river, for the owner saw the item being taken and gives up hope of recovery, i.e., we can understand why the property is considered to be that of the person who either acquired it from the thief or recovered it from the Jordan. Since the original owner was aware of his loss, he has relinquished his title and the property is therefore acquirable.

אלא גנב, מי קא חזי ליה דמיאש?—But as regards the case of the thief, has the owner seen that the property was taken and therefore given up hope of recovery? Since the owner was unaware that the property had been stolen when the person acquired it from the thief, he has not yet relinquished his claim to the property. How then can it become the property of the person who received it from the thief? However, since this *tosefta* rules that it is the property of the person who received it from the thief, we must assume that since he will give up hope of recovery once he learns that it has been stolen, it can be acquired even before he is aware of the fact that it is no longer in his possession. This would seem to support Rava and be problematic for Abbaye.

תרגמא רב פפא, בלסטים מזוין.—Rav Pappa explained that the *tosefta* was referring to a case of armed robbers; i.e., the owner was aware of the fact that the property was no longer in his possession.

אי הכי, היינו גזלן?—If this is so; i.e., if you contend that the *tosefta* is referring to a case of armed robbers, then the rulings concerning property taken by a thief and that taken by a robber are one and the same and redundant?

תרי גווני גזלן.—The reference is to two types of robbers, e.g., either armed or unarmed robbers. In both cases, the owner is considered to have relinquished his claim since he was aware of the loss. However, if he was not aware of the theft—e.g., if it had been stolen without his knowledge—then, according to Abbaye, the property would not be acquirable by the person who received it from the thief. Based on Rav Pappa's explanation of the *tosefta,* the Talmud concludes that the latter is not referring to property taken without the owner's knowledge.

תא שמע, שטף נהר קוריו עציו ואבניו ונתנו בתוך שדה חבירו, הרי אלו שלו, מפני שנתייאשו הבעלים.—Come and hear, if the river washed away a person's boards, wood, and stones and deposited them into someone else's field, they are his—i.e., the person in whose field they ended up—because the owner has given up hope of recovery.

According to Tosafos, the text should be emended to read אם נתיאשו הבעלים—*if* the owner has given up hope of recovery, rather than מפני שנתיאשו הבעלים—*because* the owner has given up hope. By emending the text to read אם—if—we see that there is a condition that enables the finder to acquire the property. It must be obvious from the owner's reaction that he has no hope of recovery—e.g., if he made no effort to recover them even though he could have done so without great effort. According to Tosafos, if the case had been talking about a situation where recovery was impossible (as would be the indication were the text to read מפני—because), this case would be no different than the case of one whose property had been washed away by the tides or currents, which had already been mentioned. In that latter case, we had already determined that both Abbaye and Rava agreed that the item was considered to be ownerless immediately, for the Torah stated that the requirement of returning a lost item applied only to something that could be seen as being recoverable.

טעמא דנתיאשו הבעלים, הא סתמא לא?—The reason why the property is considered to belong to the person in whose field it ended up is because we know that the owner has given up hope of recovery. But if we did not know that he had given up hope, it would not belong to the owner of the field. This would seem to present a problem for Rava, for according to his opinion, we do not need to know that the owner has given up hope of recovery. It is sufficient to determine this particular later.

הכא במאי עסקינן, כשיכול להציל.—This case is referring to a situation where it was possible for the owner to recover it. Since it was feasible for him to recover the property washed away, we cannot assume that he has given up hope of recovery until we know that he has indeed done so. Rashi explains that the case is similar to the loss of an item that has an identifying sign. In that situation, Rava agrees that we cannot presume that the owner will give up hope of recovery since he has a means of recovering the lost item. In this case also, since the owner can recover the items washed into the river, we cannot assume that he has given up hope of recovery. Thus, we can only rule that the property belongs to the person in whose field it ended up if we in fact know that the original owner has abandoned hope.

אי הכי, אימא סיפא.—If so—i.e., if you contend that the case is referring to a situation wherein the owner can recover the property—let us examine the last statement of this *tosefta*.

אם היו הבעלים מרדפין אחריהם, חייב להחזיר.—If the owner was chasing after the property, it must be returned, i.e., the *tosefta* specifically states that the requirement to return the property is contingent upon our seeing that the owner had made an attempt to recover it.

אי ביכולין להציל, מאי אריא מרדפין, אפילו אין מרדפין נמי?—If the case of the *tosefta* is referring to a situation wherein the owner can recover the property, what difference does it make if he was chasing after the property? Even if he was not chasing after the property, it cannot be assumed that he has given up hope of recovery.

Rashi explains that even though he is not attempting to recover the property—as evidenced by the fact that he is not chasing after the washed-away items—we cannot take his lack of action as indication of his having given up hope. It is not unlikely that the owner feels that he will be able to recover the property later. Thus, the *tosefta*'s first ruling that the items only become the property of the owner of the field if we actually know that the original owner has given up hope of recovery is still problematic for Rava. According to his opinion, there was no need to qualify the latter statement as only applying to a case where the owner had actually chased the items. Rather, if the items were recoverable, the finder could not acquire title to the items. The fact that the *tosefta* did qualify the later statement would seem to indicate that the first statement could not have been referring to a situation wherein the property was recoverable. If that first case had not been referring to such a situation, why then—according to Rava—was the finder's ability to claim the property contingent upon our knowing that the original owner had given up hope?

הכא במאי עסקינן ביכולין להציל על ידי הדחק. מרדפין לא אייאוש. לא מרדפין אייאושי מייאש.—Rather, the *tosefta*'s second ruling is referring to a situation wherein the original owner can only save his property with effort. If he chases after the property, it shows that he has not given up hope. If he does not chase after the property, it indicates that he has given up hope.

Rava explained that since recovery entailed effort, if the owner had not chased after the property immediately, we would assume that he had immediately given up hope of recovery. Thus, according to Rava, the *tosefta*'s later statement should be seen as a qualification of the former; i.e., if an item is easily recoverable, it only becomes the finder's property if we know that the original owner has given up hope. However, if recovery entails effort, then the items would become the finder's unless the original owner immediately attempted to recover them.

תא שמע, כיצד אמרו התורם שלא מדעת תרומתו תרומה?—Come and hear, how is it that they said that if one separates *terumah* without the knowledge of the owner of the produce, the separation is efficacious? Under what circumstances can *terumah* be separated and given to a *kohen* without the owner's knowledge?

הרי שירד לתוך שדה חבירו, וליקט ותרם שלא ברשות,—If a person went into his neighbor's field and gathered produce and separated *terumah* without having had permission from the owner. Rashi notes that the person went into the field for the purpose of acting on the owner's behalf.

אם חושש משום גזל, אין תרומתו תרומה. ואם לאו, תרומתו תרומה.—If the owner suspects the person of stealing, then the separation of *teru-*

mah is not efficacious. But if not—i.e., if the owner does not suspect this person of stealing—then the separation of *terumah* is efficacious.

מנין הוא יודע אם חושש משום גזל ואם לאו?—How does the person who went to gather produce know whether the owner suspects him of stealing or not?

הרי שבא בעל הבית ומצאו ואמר לו, כלך אצל יפות.—The case is referring to a situation wherein the owner of the field saw him separating *terumah* and instructed him, "pick the nicer produce."

אם נמצאו יפות מהן, תרומתו תרומה. ואם לאו, אין תרומתו תרומה.—If there is nicer produce, then the portion that he separated is *terumah*. But if there is no nicer produce, then the portion that he separated is not *terumah*.

The commentaries explain that the owner's statement, "pick the nicer produce," can be interpreted in one of two ways. If there is indeed finer produce than that which the person had separated, the statement can be seen as indicating that the owner has shown his acceptance of the action. If there is no finer produce, however, the owner's statement must be seen as being a sarcastic remark and indicative of his displeasure.

ליקטו הבעלים והוסיפו עליהן, בין כך ובין כך תרומתו תרומה.—If the owner joined with him and added to the produce that the person had separated for *terumah*, then in either case—i.e., whether there was finer produce or not—the separation is efficacious.

וכי נמצאו יפות מהן תרומתו תרומה? ואמאי, בעידנא דתרם הא לא הוה ידע?—And if there was nicer produce, the separation is efficacious; i.e., why does the *beraisa* rule that the separation is effective since the owner's statement is interpreted to mean that he has shown his acceptance? Why is this so, for when the person separated the *terumah*, the owner was unaware of the fact that he was doing so? This *beraisa* would seem to be supporting Rava's contention that a later clarification could be seen as being retroactively effective. According to Abbaye, however, the ruling would seem to be problematic, for at the time when the *terumah* was separated we were unaware of the owner's intentions. Rashi explains that in the case of *terumah* we rule that once we know that the owner accepts the action, we can retroactively apply his agreement to the time when *terumah* was separated. We should logically rule the same way as concerns lost property—i.e., since he will give up hope of recovery once he realizes that the property is lost, that giving up of hope already applies from the time that the property was lost.

תרגמה רבא אליבא דאביי דשויה שליח.—Rava explained the *beraisa* according to Abbaye, i.e., he offered a means of showing that the law cited was consistent with Abbaye's opinion and did not necessarily prove his contention. He said that the *beraisa* was referring to a case wherein the owner had appointed the person who separated the *terumah* as an agent to act on his behalf.

Thus, the person who separated the *terumah* had not acted without the owner's permission, and our later determination that the owner had agreed cannot be seen as having retroactively made the separation effective. Rather, the question that the *beraisa* had dealt with was whether the owner had intended to separate that type of produce or not. Hence, the efficacy of the separation is dependent upon there being nicer produce only to the extent of our being able to judge whether the agent had exceeded the limits of his agency or not. If there is nicer produce, then the agent can be seen as having acted according to the owner's will. If there is no nicer produce, then the agent is considered to have exceeded the limits of his agency and his separation is therefore ineffective.

הבי נמי מסתברא, דאי סלקא דעתך דלא שויה שליח, מי הויא תרומתו תרומה?—It is also logical to say that the case is referring to a case of agency, for if the owner had not appointed the person as an agent to act on his behalf, how could the separation be effective?

והא אתם גם אתם אמר רחמנא לרבות שלוחכם.—The Torah (*Bamidbar* 18:28) states: *and also you shall separate* terumah, the phrase *and also you* having been explained as granting efficacy to the separation of *terumah* by an agent.

מה אתם לדעתכם, אף שלוחכם לדעתנם—Just as your separation of *terumah* must be with your agreement, so must your agent's separation be with your agreement. Rashi points out that an agent's ability to act on the owner's behalf is limited to his acting in the same manner as the owner. Thus, just as the owner's separation of *terumah* is only effective if he separates it willingly, the agent's separation is also so limited. Hence, the separation can only be effective if the agent had been appointed to act. If he had done so without the owner being aware—i.e., if he had not been appointed an agent—the separation would be ineffective.

According to the explanation offered by Rava, the *beraisa*'s original statement, "without having had permission from the owner," must be referring to the type of produce separated rather than to the act of separation. As we have seen, the *beraisa* is referring to a case where the person had been appointed as the owner's agent.

ואמר ליה זיל תרום ולא אמר ליה תרום מהני.—The owner had told the agent "go and separate *terumah*," but did not specify from which grade of produce *terumah* should be separated.

וסתמיה דבעל הבית כי תרום, מבינונית הוא תרום—Normally, when the owner himself separates *terumah*, he separates from the middle grade of produce.

ואזל איהו ותרם מיפות—But the agent went and separated *terumah* from the better grade of produce.

ובא בעל הבית ומצאו, ואמר ליה, כלך אצל יפות.—And the owner came and saw his agent separating *terumah* and said to him, "pick from the nicer produce."

אם נמצאו יפות מהן, תרומתו תרומה. ואם לאו, אין תרומתו תרומה.—

Therefore, if there is better produce than that from which the agent separated the *terumah,* his separation is efficacious. And if not, his separation is not efficacious.

As we have already seen, the interpretation of the owner's intent is dependent upon the type of *terumah* separated. If there is better produce, we see the statement as indicating that the owner had intended to separate *terumah* from the better grade of produce. Consequently, the agent's actions on his behalf can be seen as having been according to his desires. If there is no better produce, however, the owner's statement must be seen as being a sarcastic remark and indicative that he had never intended to separate *terumah* from the better grade of produce. Hence the agent cannot be seen as having acted according to the owner's desires and the separation is therefore not efficacious.

אמימר ומר זוטרא ורב אשי אקלעו לבוסתנא דמרי בר איסק.—Ameimar, Mar Zutra, and R. Ashi once happened to come into Mari bar Isak's orchard.

אייתי אריסיה תמרי ורימוני ושדא קמייהו.—Mari bar Isak's sharecropper brought dates and pomegranates and placed them before them.

אמימר ורב אשי אכלי, מר זוטרא לא אכיל.—Ameimar and R. Ashi ate while Mar Zutra did not eat. Rashi explains that Mar Zutra held that since the owner was unaware of what the sharecropper had done, the fruit could not be eaten, for doing so would constitute theft from the owner.

Tosafos further explains that since a sharecropper has ownership rights to a portion of the produce, Ameimar and R. Ashi ate, for they held that the fruits that the sharecropper had given them were from his portion. Mar Zutra, however, was afraid that the sharecropper would not tell the owner that he had given the rabbis fruit when the produce would later be divided.

אתא מרי בר איסק אשכחינהו, ואמר ליה לאריסיה, אמאי לא אייתית להו לרבנן מהנך שופרתא?—Mari bar Isak came and found them and said to his sharecropper, "Why didn't you bring the rabbis from these better fruits?"

אמרו ליה אמימר ורב אשי למר זוטרא, השתא אמאי לא אכיל מר? והתניא! אם נמצאו יפות מהן תרומתו תרומה.—Ameimar and R. Ashi said to Mar Zutra, "Now that you have heard what Mari bar Isak said, why do you not eat? Did we not learn in a *beraisa* that if there is better produce, the separation of *terumah* is efficacious?" Rashi points out that just as that statement was taken to indicate the owner's agreement with his agent's action vis-à-vis the separation of *terumah,* so too should it be taken as indicating that the owner agreed to his sharecropper's giving the rabbis fruit. Thus, there was no reason for Mar Zutra to refuse to eat.

אמר להו, הכי אמר רבא, לא אמר כלך אצל יפות אלא לענין תרומה בלבד.— Mar Zutra replied that the *beraisa* regarding the separation of *terumah* could not be brought as support, for Rava had explained that the interpretation of the statement "pick from the nicer produce" as being indicative of the owner's retroactive agreement only applied to the separation of *terumah*.

משום דמצוה היא וניחא ליה. אבל הכא, משום כיסופא הוא דאמר הכי.— As regards *terumah,* we can assume that the owner's statement indicates his retroactive approval because the separation of *terumah* is a *mitzvah*. Therefore we can assume that the owner is willing to retroactively approve the separation of better-grade produce by his agent. However, in our case, we cannot view his statement as retroactively showing his approval, for it is likely that he only asked his sharecropper "why did you not give the rabbis from the better fruit" because he was embarrassed.

The Talmud quotes the incident of the three rabbis and the sharecropper even though it sheds no light on the disagreement between Abbaye and Rava. However, since the disagreement between Mar Zutra and R. Ashi and Ameimar is relevant to the question of separating *terumah* without the owner's knowledge, the Talmud saw fit to mention it immediately following the quotation of the *tosefta* regarding *terumah*. Having clarified the reason for Mar Zutra's refusal to eat, the Talmud returns to its original discussion.

תא שמע עודהו הטל עליהן ושמח, הרי זה בכי יתן.—Come and hear, if the dew is still on the fruit and he—the owner—was happy, they are considered to be in the status of having had water been put on them.

The Torah (*Vayikra* 11:38) states: *and when water is put on a plant, and it then comes into contact with a corpse, it is ritually impure,* i.e., plants can only become ritually impure after they have been dampened. The *tosefta* rules that dew can be considered to have wetted the plant in terms of the laws of ritual impurity if the owner of the fruit, upon discovering them covered by dew, is happy that they were dampened since the dew will keep them fresh.

It should be noted that the owner's being happy—i.e., agreeable—is one of the preconditions for the produce being able to become ritually impure.

נגבו, אף על פי ששמח, אינן בכי יתן.—If they had dried out before he found them, then even though he was happy that they had been wetted by the dew, they are not considered to have been wetted vis-à-vis ritual impurity.

As the Talmud proceeds to explain, this *halachah* would seem to be problematic to Rava. According to his opinion that a later clarification can be seen as having retroactive effect, the *halachah* in the case of where he found that the dew had dried should have been that the plants were considered to have been wetted since he was happy that they had been dampened by the dew. Thus, the fact that he has now indicated that he is agreeable should be seen as if he was agreeable while they were still wet—even though he was unaware of their status at that time.

טעמא מאי? לאו משום דלא אמרינן כיון דאיגלאי מילתא דהשתא ניחא ליה מעיקרא נמי ניחא ליה.—What is the reason why we do not consider them to have been wetted if he found them dry? Is it not because we do not say that his being happy now is not retroactively applied to indicate that he was happy when they were still wet?

According to Rava, it should make no difference that the fruit is now dry. Since we know that he is happy that the dew had wetted them, we should say that it is *as if* he was happy while they were still wet. The fact that we do not say so would seem to indicate that the *tosefta* supports Abbaye's view.

שאני התם, דכתיב כי יתן–עד שיתן.—That case is different, for the Torah says *and when water is put on a plant,* which is understood to mean that they can only become ritually impure if the plants are wetted with his knowledge. If the owner found them after they had dried, they could not become ritually impure based on their having been wet, for even though the owner was glad that they had been wetted, he was unaware of the fact that they had been dampened while they were still wet, a condition that the Torah had made in this case.

The word יתן has a *shuruk* under the י, which means *is placed*. However, inasmuch as the Torah has no vowels, the word could also be read as יתן with a *chirik* under the י, which would change the meaning to *he places,* i.e., when the produce is wetted with his knowledge. The Talmud explains that the two ways of reading the word come to teach us that the produce—in order to be able to become ritually impure—must be wetted in a manner that can meet the criterion of *he places,* i.e., it can only become ritually impure if they were wetted in a manner that is similar to his having wetted them himself—with his knowledge. Because the Torah had specified this law vis-à-vis ritual impurity, one cannot draw inferences regarding other retroactive decisions. This case was a specific Torah decree applying only to ritual impurity.

אי הכי, רישא נמי?—If this is so, then the *tosefta*'s first statement should be the same. How can you claim that the Torah had specifically decreed that plants could only become ritually impure if the owner was aware of the fact that they had been wetted, when the first statement of the *tosefta* rules that they can become ritually impure if the owner found them while they were still wet? In that case the owner had not wetted the produce himself, he had only found them while they were still wet!

התם כדרב פפא, דרב פפא רמי, כתיב כי יתן, וקרינן כי יותן. הא כיצד? בעינן כי יותן דומיא דכי יתן. מה יתן לדעת, אף כי יותן לדעת.—That—the first statement—is as explained by Rav Pappa. For Rav Pappa questioned: The verse is written כי יתן—*when he places*—but is read כי יותן—*when it is placed*. How is this possible, i.e., how is it possible to reconcile the way the word is written, which implies that the owner must wet the produce, with the way the word is read, which implies that the produce can become ritually impure even if it became wet by itself? The answer is that we require that it become wet in the same manner as if he had wetted it, i.e., just as the latter requires his foreknowledge, so too does the former require his foreknowledge.

Rashi explains that when the produce is still wet from the dew, it is as if it had been wetted with the owner's knowledge, for now when he finds them they are in fact wet. Therefore, they can become ritually impure. However, if they had already dried when he found them, then the fact that they had been previously wet would be of no avail since he was not aware of the fact that they were wet when they were in fact dampened.

The explanation of R. Pappa would seem to be a refinement of the earlier statement that had sought to reconcile the ruling of Rava with the *halachah* of the *tosefta*. In both cases, the Talmud explains that the *halachah* of ritual impurity is a unique situation; i.e., the Torah had specified that foreknowledge was required. Rava would also agree that his contention that the owner's later giving up hope of recovery was *as if* he had already given up hope at the time of loss would not apply in this case. Since the Torah required foreknowledge—as the verse indicates—a retrospective *as if* could not be seen as being equivalent.

תא שמע, דאמר רבי יוחנן משום רבי ישמעל בן יהוצדק. מנין לאבידה ששטפה נהר שהיא מותרת?—Come and hear, R.Yochanan taught in the name of R.Yishmael ben Yehotzadak: How do we know that if an item was washed away by the river that it is permitted, i.e., that the finder need not announce its discovery but may keep it?

דכתיב וכן תעשה לחמורו וכן תעשה לשמלתו וכן תעשה לכל אבידת אחיך אשר תאבד ממנו ומצאתה.—The verse (*Devarim* 22:3) states: *You shall do so [i.e., return the lost property] for his donkey, and you shall do so for his garment and you shall do so for all things which your brother has lost and which you found.*

מי שאבודה הימנו ומצויה אצל כל אדם—Something that is lost to the owner but can be found by anyone else, i.e., the verse requiring one to return lost property refers to an item that can potentially be found by anyone.

יצאתה זו שאבודה הימנו ואינה מצויה אצל כל אדם—But this would not include this—i.e., an item that had been washed away in the river—which is considered to have been lost by the owner and is not potentially findable by anyone. R.Yochanan explained that the wording of the verse limited the obligation of returning lost property to that which was potentially discoverable by anyone. If the property had been washed away in the river, it should be viewed as being just as lost to the potential finders as it is to the owner. Therefore, the finder is not obligated to return it.

ואיסורא דומיא דהיתרא—And no differentiation is made between a prohibited case—i.e., a loss that must be returned—and a permitted case—i.e., a loss that may be kept by the finder. Rashi explains that since the requirement to return some types of losses and the permission to keep others is derived from the same verse, we cannot rule that the two cases refer to different circumstances.

מה היתרא, בין דאית בה סימן ובין דלית בה סימן, שרא—Just as in the case of discoveries that need not be announced—i.e., when the item was washed into the water—no differentiation is made between an item that has an identifying sign and one that does not have an identifying sign and both may be kept by the finder.

אף איסורא, בין דאית בה סימן בין דלית ביה סימן, אסורה.—So too is the *halachah* as concerns losses that must be returned. Whether they have an identifying sign or not, they are prohibited; i.e., if the finder keeps them rather than attempting to return them he is considered to have acquired the property in a prohibited fashion.

Again, we find the Talmud using the term איסורא—prohibited. Since the finder was obligated to return the item, failure to do so renders him a thief.

תיובתא דרבא תיובתא.—This is a question for which Rava can offer no answer.

According to the *beraisa* cited, there could not be a requirement to return an object that has no identifying sign, for how could one know that he had returned it to the rightful owner? Rather, the *beraisa* maintains that the prohibition of taking a discovered item for oneself is not dependent upon its having an identifying sign. It is dependent upon the owner's having given up hope of recovery. Once he does so, the finder may keep the item for he has acquired an ownerless object. According to Rava, however, if there was no identifying sign, the item should have been considered ownerless from the time that it was lost. Why then did the *beraisa* not differentiate between an item that has an identifying sign and one that does not? The fact that it did not indicates that it did not accept Rava's viewpoint.

Tosafos points out that there was no need for a verse to teach us that the finder may keep the discovered item if the owner has given up hope of recovery before the finder found the item. This would be obvious, for the item is ownerless once hope has been given up. Rather, the verse teaches us that if the item came into the finder's hands before the owner had given up hope, we would consider it as if the item had come into his hands in a prohibited manner. The owner's later *yiush* would be of no avail since the finder had acquired the property while it was still prohibited. Clearly, it is the giving up of hope that makes the item acquirable by the finder—not the loss as Rava had contended. Thus the *beraisa*'s explanantion of the verse stands in direct contrast to Rava's opinion.

והלכתא כוותיה דאביי ביע"ל קג"ם.—And the *halachah* is in accordance with Abbaye in six of the disputes that he had with Rava—including this dispute. יעל קגם is an acronym; each letter representing a subject that was disputed by Abbaye and Rava.

Appendix I
Divisions of the Talmud

The following is a list of the tractates that make up the six orders of the Talmud. Students might come across references to the existence of sixty tractates, rather than the sixty-three listed; originally, *Sanhedrin* and *Makkos* were a single tractate, as were the three *Bavas* in *Seder Nezikin.* The *tosefta* that has come down to us covers all of the tractates except for *Avos, Tamid, Middos,* and *Kinnim.* The *tosefta* of *Kellim* is divided into three, also referred to as *Bava Kamma, Bava Metzia,* and *Bava Basra.*

	Tractate	*Bavli*	*Yerushalmi*
Zera'im	*Berachos*	•	•
	Pe'ah	Mishnah only	•
	Demai	Mishnah only	•
	Kilayim	Mishnah only	•
	Shvi'is	Mishnah only	•
	Terumos	Mishnah only	•
	Ma'asros	Mishnah only	•
	Ma'aser Sheni	Mishnah only	•
	Challah	Mishnah only	•
	Orlah	Mishnah only	•
	Bikkurim	Mishnah only	•

	Tractate	Bavli	Yerushalmi
Mo'ed	*Shabbos*	•	•
	Eruvin	•	•
	Pesachim	•	•
	Shekalim	Mishnah only	•
	Yuma	•	•
	Sukkah	•	•
	Betzah	•	•
	Rosh Hashanah	•	•
	Ta'anis	•	•
	Megillah	•	•
	Mo'ed Katan	•	•
Nashim	*Yevamos*	•	•
	Kesubos	•	•
	Nedarim	•	•
	Nazir	•	•
	Sotah	•	•
	Gittin	•	•
	Kiddushin	•	•
Nezikin	*Bava Kamma*	•	•
	Bava Metzia	•	•
	Bava Basra	•	•
	Sanhedrin	•	•
	Makkos	•	•
	Shevu'os	•	•
	Eduyos	Mishnah only	•
	Avodah Zarah	•	•
	Avos	Mishnah only	•
	Horios	•	•

	Tractate	*Bavli*	*Yerushalmi*
Kodshim	*Zevachim*	•	—
	Menachos	•	—
	Chullin	•	—
	Bechoros	•	—
	Arachin	•	—
	Temurah	•	—
	Krisos	•	—
	Me'ilah	•	—
	Tamid	•	—
	Middos	Mishnah only	—
	Kinnim	Mishnah only	—
Taharos	*Kelim*	Mishnah only	—
	Oholos	Mishnah only	—
	Nega'im	Mishnah only	—
	Parah	Mishnah only	—
	Taharos	Mishnah only	—
	Mikva'os	Mishnah only	—
	Niddah	•	*partial*
	Machshirin	Mishnah only	—
	Zavim	Mishnah only	—
	T'vul Yom	Mishnah only	—
	Yadayim	Mishnah only	—
	Uktzin	Mishnah only	—

Appendix II

Divisions of the *Yad ha-Chazakah*

The following is a list of the divisions that the Rambam used in his *Yad ha-Chazakah* along with the *halachos* included in each division.

א–מדע
יסודי התורה
דעות
תלמוד תורה
עבודת כוכבים
תשובה

ב–אהבה
קריאת שמע
תפילה וברכת כהנים
תפילין, מזוזות
וספר תורה
ציצית
ברכות
מילה

ג–זמנים
שבת
עירובין
שביתת עשור
שביתת יום טוב
חמץ ומצה
שופר, סוכה ולולב
שקלים
קדוש החדש
תענית
מגילה וחנוכה

ד–נשים
אישות
גירושין
יבום וחליצה
נערה בתולה
סוטה

ה–קדושה
איסורי ביאה
מאכלות אסורות
שחיטה

ו–הפלאה
שבועות
נדרים
נזירות
ערכין וחרמין

ז–זרעים
כלאים
מתנות עניים
תרומות
מעשרות
מעשר שני ונטע רבעי

ז–זרעים
בכורים ומתנות כהונה
שמטה ויובל

ח–עבודה
בית הבחירה
כלי המקדש
ביאת המקדש
איסורי המזבח
מעשה הקרבנות
תמידין ומוספין
פסולי המוקדשין
עבודת יום הכפורים
מעילה

ט–קרבנות
קרבן פסח
חגיגה
בכורות
שגגות

ט–קרבנות
מחוסרי כפרה
תמורה

י–טהרה
טומאת מת
פרה אדומה
טומאת צרעת
משכב ומושב
אבות הטומאה
טומאת אוכלין
כלים
מקוואות

יא–נזיקין
נזקי ממון
גנבה
גזלה ואבדה
חובל ומזיק
רוצח ושמירת הנפש

יב–קנין
מכירה
זכיה ומתנה
שכנים
שלוחין ושותפין
עבדים

יג–משפטים
שכירות
שאלה ופקדון
מלוה ולוה
טוען ונטען
נחלות

יד–שופטים
סנהדרין
עדות
ממרים
אבל
מלכים

The following is an alphabetical list of the *halachos* and the divisions in which they appear.

ספר	הלכה
טהרה	אבות הטומאה
שופטים	אבל
קדושה	איסורי ביאה
עבודה	איסורי המזבח
נשים	אישות
עבודה	ביאת המקרש
עבודה	בית הבחירה
קרבנות	בכורות
זרעים	בכורים ומתנות כהונה
אהבה	ברכות
נשים	גירושין
נזיקין	גנבה
נזיקין	גזלה ואבדה
מדע	דעות
קנין	זכיה ומתנה
קרבנות	חגיגה
נזיקין	חובל ומזיק
זמנים	חמץ ומצה
זמנים	חנוכה
טהרה	טומאת אוכלין
טהרה	טומאת מת
טהרה	טומאת צרעת
משפטים	טוען ונטען
נשים	יבום וחליצה
מדע	יסודי התורה
זרעים	כלאים
טהרה	כלים
עבודה	כלי המקדש

ספר	הלכה
קדושה	מאכלות אסורות
זמנים	מגילה
קרבנות	מחוסרי כפרה
אהבה	מילה
קנין	מכירה
משפטים	מלוה ולוה
שופטים	מלכים
שופטים	ממרים
עבודה	מעילה
עבודה	מעשה הקרבנות
זרעים	מעשרות
זרעים	מעשר שני ונטע רבעי
טהרה	מקוואות
טהרה	משכב ומושב
זרעים	מתנות עניים
הפלאה	נדרים
הפלאה	נזירות
נזיקין	נזקי ממון
משפטים	נחלות
אישות	נערה בתולה
שופטים	סנהדרין
קנין	עבדים
עבודה	עבודת יום הכפורים
מדע	עבודת כוכבים
שופטים	עדות
זמנים	עירובין
הפלאה	ערכין וחרמין
עבודה	פסולי המוקדשין

ספר	הלכה
טהרה	פרה אדומה
אהבה	ציצית
זמנים	קדוש החדש
אהבה	קריאת שמע
נזיקין	רוצח ושמירת הנפש
משפטים	שאלה ופקדון
הפלאה	שבועות
זמנים	שביתת יום טוב
זמנים	שביתת עשור
זמנים	שבת
קרבנות	שגגות
זמנים	שופר, סוכה ולולב
קדושה	שחיטה

ספר	הלכה
משפטים	שכירות
קנין	שכנים
קנין	שלוחין ושותפין
זרעים	שמטה ויובל
זמנים	שקלים
אהבה	תלמוד תורה
קרבנות	תמורה
קרבנות	תמידין ומוספין
זמנים	תענית
אהבה	תפילה וברכת כהנים
אהבה	תפילין, מזוזות וספר תורה
זרעים	תרומות
מדע	תשובה

Appendix III
Divisions of *Shulchan Aruch*

The following is a list of the *halachos* brought in *Shulchan Aruch* arranged according to the order in which they appear.

מסימן עד סימן	הלכות
אורח חיים	
א	הנהגת אדם בבקר
ב	לבישת בגדים
ג	הנהגת בית הכסא
ד-ז	נטילת ידים (בבקר)
י-כד	ציצית
כה-מה	תפילין
מו-נז	ברכות (תפלה)
נח-פט	קריאת שמע (שחרית)
צ-קכז	תפלה (עד מודים)
קכח-קל	נשיאת כפים (ברכת כהנים)
קלא	נפילת אפים (תחנון)
קלב-קלד	תפילה (סוף)
קלה-קמט	קריאת התורה
קנ-קנה	בית הכנסת

מסימן עד סימן	הלכות
אורח חיים	
קנו	משא ומתן
קנז-קסו	נטילת ידים (לאוכל)
קסו-קסח	נציעת הפת
קסט-קפ	סעודה
קפא	מים אחרונים
קפב-רא	ברכת המזון
רב-רלא	ברכות (שאר ברכות)
רלב-רלד	מנחה
רלה-רלט	קריאת שמע (ערבית/על המטה)
רמ-רמא	צניעות
רמב-שצו	שבת
שצז-תטז	עירוב תחומין
תיז-תכח	ראש חדש
תכט-תצב	פסח

מסימן עד סימן	הלכות
אורח חיים	
תצג	הנהגת ימי העומר
תצד	חג השבועות
תצה-תקכט	יום טוב
תקל-תקמח	חול המועד
תקמט-תקסא	ט׳ באב
תקסב-תקפ	תענית
תקפא-תרג	ראש השנה
תרד-תרכד	יום כפור
תרכה-תרמד	סוכה
תרמה-תרסט	לולב
תרע-תרפה	חנוכה
תרפו-תרצז	מגילה (פורים)
יורה דעה	
א-כח	שחיטה
כט-ס	טריפות
ס-סא	מתנות כהונה
סב	אבר מן החי
סג	בשר שנתעלם מן העין
סד-	חלבים
סה-סח	דם
סט-עח	מליחה
עט-פ	בהמה וחיה טהורה
פא	דברים היוצאים מן החי
פב	עופות
פג	דגים
פד	תולעים
פה	חגבים

מסימן עד סימן	הלכות
יורה דעה	
פו	ביצים
פז-צז	בשר בחלב
צח-קיא	תערובות
קיב-קיט	מאכלי עכו״ם
קכ-קכב	הכשרת כלים
קכב	נותן טעם
קכג-קלח	יין נסך
קלט-קנט	עבודת כוכבים
קנט-קעז	רובית
קעח-קפ	חוקות הגוים
קפא	גילוח
קפב	לא ילבש
קפג-ר	נדה
רא-רב	מקוואות
רג-רלט	נדרים
רמ-רמא	כבוד אב ואם
רמב-רמד	כבוד רבו ות״ח
רמה	מלמדים
רמו	תלמוד תורה
רמז-רנט	צדקה
רס-רסו	מילה
רסז	עבדים
רסח-רסט	גרים
ער-רפד	ספר תורה
רפה-רצא	מזוזה
רצב	שלוח הקן
רצג	חדש
רצד	ערלה
רצה-רצז	כלאים
רצח-שד	שעטנז

מסימן עד סימן	הלכות
יורה דעה	
שו-שכא	פדיון בכור בהמה
שכב-של	חלה
שלא-שלג	תרומות ומעשרות
שלד	נידוי וחרם
שלה-שלט	ביקור חולים
שמ-תג	אבילות
שה	פדיון בכור אדם
אבן העזר	
א-ו	פריה ורביה
ז-כה	אישות
כו-סה	קדושין
סו-קיח	כתובות
קיט-קנד	גיטין
קנה	מיאון
קנו-קע	יבום וחליצה
חשן משפט	
א-כז	דיינים
כח-לח	עדות
לט-עד	הלואה
עה-צו	טוען ונטען
צז-קו	גביית מלוה
קז-קי	גביית חוב מיתומים
קיא-קטז	גביית חוב מנכסים
קטז-קכ	אפותיקי
קכא-	גביה ע"י שליח
קכב-קכח	הרשאה
קכט-קלב	ערב

מסימן עד סימן	הלכות
חשן משפט	
קלג-קלט	חזקת מטלטלין
קמ-קנב	חזקת קרקעות
קנג-קנו	נזקי שכנים
קנז-קע	שותפים בקרקע
קעא-קעה	חלוקת שותפות
קעו-קפא	שותפים
קפב-קפח	שלוחין
קפט-רכו	מקח וממכר
רכז-רמ	אונאה ומקח טעות
רמא-רמט	מתנה
רנ-רנח	מתנת שכיב מרע
רנט-רעא	אבידה ומציאה
רעב	פריקה וטעינה
רעג-ערה-	הפקר ונכסי הגר
רעו-רפט	נחלות
רצ	אפיטרופוס
רצא-שב	פקדון
שג-שו	שומר שכר
שז-שיט	שוכר
שכ-של	חכירות וקבלנות
שלא-שלט	שכירת פועלים
שמ-שמז	שאלה
שמח-שנח	גניבה
שנט-שעז	גזילה
שעח-שפז	נזיקין
שפז-שפח	מאבד ממון חבירו ומסירה
שפט-תיט	נזקי ממון
תכ-תכו	חובל בחבירו
תכז	שמירת הנפש

The following is a list of the *halachos* arranged in alphabetical order.

מסימן עד סימן	חלק	הלכות
רנט-רעא	ח״מ	אבידה ומציאה
שמ-תג	יו״ד	אבילות
סב	יו״ד	אבר מן החי
רכז-רמ	ח״מ	אונאה ומקח טעות
ז-כה	אה״ע	אישות
קיז-קכ	ח״מ	אפותיקי
רצ	ח״מ	אפיטרופוס
עט-פ	יו״ד	בהמה וחיה טהורה
פו	יו״ד	ביצים
שלה-שלט	יו״ד	ביקור חולים
קנ-קנה	או״ח	בית הכנסת
קסו-קסח	או״ח	בציעת הפת
פז-צו	יו״ד	בשר בחלב
רב-רלא	או״ח	ברכות (שאר ברכות)
מו-נז	או״ח	ברכות (תפלה)
קפב-רא	או״ח	ברכת המזון
סג	יו״ד	בשר שנתעלם מן העין
קכא-	ח״מ	גביה ע״י שליח
קז-קי	ח״מ	גביית חוב מיתומים
קיא-קטז	ח״מ	גביית חוב מנכסים
צז-קו	ח״מ	גביית מלוה
שנט-שעז	ח״מ	גזילה
קיט-קנד	אה״ע	גיטין
קפא	יו״ד	גילוח
שמח-שנח	ח״מ	גניבה
רסח-רסט	יו״ד	גרים
פג	יו״ד	דגים

מסימן עד סימן	חלק	הלכות
פא	יו״ד	דברים היוצאים מן החי
סח	יו״ד	דם
א-כז	ח״מ	דיינים
קכ-קכב	יו״ד	הכשרת כלים
לט-עד	ח״מ	הלואה
א	או״ח	הנהגת אדם בבקר
ג	או״ח	הנהגת בית הכסא
תצג	או״ח	הנהגת ימי העומר
רעג-ערה-	ח״מ	הפקר ונכסי הגר
קכב-קכח	ח״מ	הרשאה
תצד	או״ח	חג השבועות
פה	יו״ד	חגבים
רצג	יו״ד	חדש
תכ-תכו	ח״מ	חובל בחבירו
תקל-תקמח	או״ח	חול המועד
קעח-קפ	יו״ד	חוקות הגוים
קלג-קלט	ח״מ	חזקת מטלטלין
קמ-קנב	ח״מ	חזקת קרקעות
שכ-של	ח״מ	חכירות וקבלנות
סד	יו״ד	חלב
קעא-קעה	ח״מ	חלוקת שותפות
שכב-של	יו״ד	חלה
תרע-תרפה	או״ח	חנוכה
תקמט-תקסא	או״ח	ט׳ באב
עה-צו	ח״מ	טוען ונטען
כט-ס	יו״ד	טריפות
קנו-קעח	אה״ע	יבום וחליצה
תצה-תקכט	או״ח	יום טוב
תרד-תרכד	או״ח	יום כפור

מסימן עד סימן	חלק	הלכות
קכג-קלח	יו"ד	יין נסך
רמ-רמא	יו"ד	כבוד אב ואם
רמב-רמד	יו"ד	כבוד רבו ות"ח
רצה-רצז	יו"ד	כלאים
סו-קיח	אה"ע	כתובות
קפב	יו"ד	לא ילבש
ב	או"ח	לבישת בגדים
תרמה-תרסט	או"ח	לולב
שפז-שפח	ח"מ	מאבד ממון חבירו ומסירה
קיב-קיט	יו"ד	מאכלי עכו"ם
תרפו-תרצז	או"ח	מגילה (פורים)
רפה-רצא	יו"ד	מזוזה
קנה	אה"ע	מיאון
רס-רסו	יו"ד	מילה
קפא	או"ח	מים אחרונים
סט-עח	יו"ד	מליחה
רמה	יו"ד	מלמדים
רלב-רלד	או"ח	מנחה
רא-רב	יו"ד	מקוואות
קפט-רכו	ח"מ	מקח וממכר
קנו	או"ח	משא ומתן
רמא-רמט	ח"מ	מתנה
ס-סא	יו"ד	מתנות כהונה
רנ-רנח	ח"מ	מתנת שכיב מרע
קפג-ר	יו"ד	נדה
רג-רלט	יו"ד	נדרים
קכב	יו"ד	נותן טעם
שעח-שפז	ח"מ	נזיקין
שפט-תיט	ח"מ	נזקי ממון

הלכות	חלק	מסימן עד סימן
נזקי שכנים	ח"מ	קנג-קנו
נחלות	ח"מ	רעו-רפט
נטילת ידים (לאוכל)	או"ח	קנז-קסו
נטילת ידים (בבקר)	או"ח	ד-ז
נידוי וחרם	יו"ד	שלד
נפילת אפים (תחנון)	או"ח	קלא
נשיאת כפים (ברכת כהנים)	או"ח	קכח-קל
סוכה	או"ח	תרכה-תרמד
סעודה	או"ח	קסט-קפ
ספר תורה	יו"ד	ער-רפד
עבדים	יו"ד	רסז
עדות	ח"מ	כח-לח
עופות	יו"ד	פב
עירוב תחומין	או"ח	שצז-תטז
ערב	ח"מ	קכט-קלב
ערלה	יו"ד	רצד
פדיון בכור אדם	יו"ד	שה
פדיון בכור בהמה	יו"ד	שו-שכא
פסח	או"ח	תכט-תצב
פקדון	ח"מ	רצא-שב
פריה ורביה	אה"ע	א-ו
פריקה וטעינה	ח"מ	רעב
צדקה	יו"ד	רמז-רנט
ציצית	או"ח	י-כד
צניעות	או"ח	רמ-רמא
קדושין	אה"ע	כו-סה
קריאת התורה	או"ח	קלה-קמט
ק"ש (ערבית/על המטה)	או"ח	רלה-רלט

הלכות	חלק	מסימן עד סימן
ק"ש (שחרית)	או"ח	נח-פט
ראש השנה	או"ח	תקפא-תרג
ראש חדש	או"ח	תיז-תכח
רבית	יו"ד	קנט-קעז
שאלה	ח"מ	שמ-שמז
שבת	או"ח	רמג-שצו
שוכר	ח"מ	שז-שיט
שומר שכר	ח"מ	שג-שו
שותפים	ח"מ	קעו-קפא
שותפים בקרקע	ח"מ	קנז-קע
שחיטה	יו"ד	א-כח
שכירת פועלים	ח"מ	שלא-שלט
שלוחין	ח"מ	קפב-קפח
שלוח הקן	יו"ד	רצב
שמירת הנפש	ח"מ	תכז
שעטנז	יו"ד	רצח-שד
תולעים	יו"ד	פד
תלמוד תורה	יו"ד	רמו-
תענית	או"ח	תקסב-תקפ
תערובות	יו"ד	צח-קיא-
תפלה (עד מודים)	או"ח	צ-קכז
תפילה (סוף)	או"ח	קלב-קלד
תפילין	או"ח	כה-מה
תרומות ומעשרות	יו"ד	שלא-שלג

Glossary

acharonim—the later masters, i.e., the rabbis and scholars who followed the *rishonim.* It is difficult to establish a specific year that begins the period of the *acharonim.* Many historians of Jewish literature see the expulsion from Spain in 1492 as marking the transition point between the two eras. As is the case with the transition from the *tanna'im* to the *amora'im,* or from the *geonim* to the *rishonim,* the new era is seen to have begun when the major talmudic academies in one area ceased to flourish and new major centers of Torah learning were established elsewhere. In this case, the yeshivos of Spain ceased to exist, and academic activity was transferred to Italy, Turkey, Eretz Yisrael, and Northern Europe. Although these latter centers predated the expulsion from Spain, they were overshadowed as long as the Spanish Torah center flourished.

aggadah/aggados—The nonhalachic portion of the Talmud and of the Midrash. *Aggadah* has two forms: nonlegal exegesis of *Tanach* that provides us with historical information and ethical and moral lessons that are independent of scriptural linkage.

agunah/agunos—literally, an anchored woman; i.e., a woman who is unable to remarry because of her inability to receive a divorce document from her husband. This status is a result of many different situations; e.g., if a woman's husband refuses to grant her a divorce, or if he is mentally incapable of writing a divorce document, or if no divorce can be granted because the husband is not present. The classic *agunah* that is dealt with at great length in halachic literature refers to a situation where the husband has disappeared during war and no testimony is available to certify that he has been killed. The concern that the rabbis have always shown for this situation might best be evidenced by the fact that during the reign of Dovid *ha-Melech,* it was customary for soldiers to grant their wives conditional divorces so as to prevent them from becoming *agunos*.

al kiddush ha-Shem—in sanctification of God's name, used primarily to describe one who has died as a martyr because of his faith.

amora/amora'im—literally, those who spoke; i.e, the rabbis and scholars who expounded upon the teachings of the *tanna'im* and whose discussions and dialogues form most of the Talmud. The period of the *amora'im* is considered to have begun with the final redaction of the Mishnah in 188 C.E. by R. Yehudah ha-Nasi. Although R. Yehudah's disciples R. Chiya and Rav were themselves still considered to be *tanna'im,* their colleagues were considered to be of lesser stature in that they were no longer permitted to disagree with the halachic rulings of a *tanna* unless they had evidence of another tannaitic opinion supporting their position. The period of the *amora'im* ended with the death of Ravina II in 475 and with the final editing of the Talmud *Bavli* around the year 500. This is referred to as *sof hora'ah*—the point at which no additional halachic material could be added to the Talmud. The Rambam (Introduction to *Yad ha-Chazakah*) writes that with the closing of the Talmud *Bavli,* no *beis din* has the authority to compel all of Jewry to follow its decrees.

Ashkenaz—Germany, but also used as a reference to the Jewish communities of Northern and Eastern Europe. In the period after the *geonim,* two separate schools of Jewish learning flourished in Europe. The Spanish community—which was founded by the Rif and the Ri mi-Gash—followed the customs of North Africa and Babylonia. The smaller Northern European community was guided by

Rabbenu Gershom. The two communities were in close contact, but through the years, diverse customs and traditions developed including different texts for prayer and differences in halachic rulings. The trend toward separate communities accelerated with the beginning of the Inquisition and the concurrent decline of the Spanish academies. It became most pronounced with the publication of the *Shulchan Aruch* of R. Yosef Caro—which followed the rulings of the Spanish schools—with the glosses of R. Moshe Isserles who based his exceptions on the rulings of the Northern European scholars; especially R. Yisrael Isserlein, the Maharil, and Maharshal.

av beis din—head of the rabbinical court. The position of *av beis din* is first found in the pretannaitic era of the *zuggos*—the pairs of scholars who headed the *Sanhedrin*. The *av beis din* served as deputy director of the court, second in stature to the *nasi*. It should be noted that the positions of *nasi* and *av beis din* were only created when the *kohen gadol* was no longer of sufficient stature to serve as head of the *Sanhedrin*—the office having become a political appointment based on the strength of various factions. In later years, the term was used for the head of local rabbinical courts established in various Jewish communities. At times these courts had broad political power as the Jews enjoyed a somewhat autonomous status and were permitted to live their lives according to *halachah*.

Avos—tractate of *mishnayos* in the order *Nezikin* that traces the transmission of the oral Torah and provides ethical sayings of the *tanna'im*.

Bava Basra—tractate in the order *Nezikin*.

Bava Kamma—tractate in the order *Nezikin*.

Bava Metzia—tractate in the order *Nezikin*. The three *Bavas* are one tractate and were only divided because of their length.

Bavli—Babylonian; specifically, the Babylonian Talmud as opposed to the Talmud of Eretz Yisrael, the *Yerushalmi*.

beis din—rabbinical court. See *av beis din*.

Beis ha-Mikdash—the Temple in Jerusalem. The first *Beis ha-Mikdash,* built by Shlomo in 832 B.C.E. (2928), stood for 410 years until it was destroyed by Nevuchadnezer on the 9th of *Av,* 422 B.C.E. (3338). The second *Beis ha-Mikdash,* built by Ezra and Nechemiah in 352 B.C.E. (3408), stood for 420 years until it was destroyed by Titus on the 9th of *Av,* 68 C.E. (3828).

Berachos—tractate in the order *Zera'im.*

beraisa/beraisos—literally outside, i.e., the collection of tannaitic statements that were left outside of the Mishnah when it was edited and set by R. Yehudah ha-Nasi. In some instances, *beraisos* include halachic statements that the Mishnah records in the name of another *tanna.* It would seem that when R. Yehudah ha-Nasi selected the statements that would form the Mishnah, he chose those statements that were the most clear and concise since his reason for establishing a set Mishnah was to provide students with a vehicle that would enable them to quickly recall and comprehend the statements of the *tanna'im.* The Talmud (*Chullin* 141b) states that the *beraisos* of R. Chiya and R. Oshiya are the most accurate collections.

challah—the portion of dough that one is required to separate and give to a *kohen* as a means of providing him with support.

chasidei Ashkenaz—literally, the pious of Germany; used to describe the school of R. Yehudah ha-Chasid (Germany—1150–1217), author of *Sefer Chasidim.* In this work, R. Yehudah outlined a lifestyle based on an extremely moral and pious code of individual behavior. The work includes a great deal of halachic material. Most editions of the *Sefer Chasidim* also include R. Yehudah's ethical will in which he outlines a number of prohibitions that are widely known, e.g., not marrying a woman whose name is the same as one's mother. Many halachic authorities maintain that R. Yehudah's will was meant for his family and followers and should not be seen as being obligatory upon others.

chasidim—literally, the pious; primarily used to describe the followers of R. Yisroel Ba'al Shem Tov and R. Dov Baer of Mezeritch.

Choshen Mishpat—one of the four divisions of *halachah,* which deals with civil law, first used in the *Tur* of R. Yaakov ben Asher and followed by R. Yosef Caro in his *Shulchan Aruch.*

Eiduyos—tractate of *mishnayos* in the order *Nezikin.*

eruv—literally, mixing. A halachic device that joins two actions or areas so that the resultant combination can take advantage of the halachic status that would be denied them were they to remain separate. There are a number of different *eruvin* that are employed. The following is a brief explanation of the different types of *eruvin* mentioned in the Talmud and halachic literature.

Please note that the proper establishment of an *eruv* requires a great deal of halachic expertise, and the following examples are meant solely as a means of helping the reader understand the concepts involved:

1. *eruv chatzeros*—The Torah proscribes carrying articles on Shabbos for four *amos*—cubits—within a public domain, which is defined either as a thoroughfare that is sixteen *amos* wide or through which 600,000 people traverse daily. Rabbinically, this prohibition was expanded to include the carrying of articles within a *karmelis*—a publicly owned thoroughfare that does not meet either of the above criteria. By constructing an *eruv chatzeros*—a fence (or a wire around the area that serves the purpose of enclosing it)—that surrounds the entire thoroughfare, one can give the area the status of a single private domain in which one is permitted to carry articles. The *eruv chatzeros* thus serves to mix the commonly owned property and establish it as a single domain.
2. *shitufei ma'vaos*—The Torah proscribes the transfer of articles from a public domain into a private domain and vice versa. Rabbinically, the transfer of articles between two separate private domains was

prohibited as a safeguard to prevent people from accidentally transferring articles between areas that the Torah had prohibited. Thus, one cannot carry articles on a staircase that opens up to many different apartments or in a yard or street that is open to many different homes even if they are completely enclosed.

Shlomo and his *beis din* established the *eruv* of *shitufei ma'vaos* to enable people to carry in these areas by linking all of those concerned so that the area can be considered to be a single private domain. Food is taken before *Shabbos,* either jointly by the people involved or by one person who acts as an agent on behalf of the others, and its ownership is transferred to all of the people who live within the area. The *shitufei ma'vaos* thus serves to mix all of the independently owned properties into one and thus permits the transfer of articles within the area.

3. *eruv tavshillin*—Although the Torah permits one to cook on festivals, one may only do so for use on the festival itself. One may not cook food that is meant for use on the day following the festival. Thus, if a festival fell on a Friday, one would be prohibited to cook food on the festival even it was meant for use on *Shabbos.* However, one can prepare food for *Shabbos* on the eve of the festival and declare that he is doing so as a means of continuing to cook on the festival itself. The food that he has prepared on the eve of the festival—the *eruv tavshillin*—is mixed with the food that he will cook on the festival so that it can be seen as a single extended act of cooking.
4. *eruv techumim*—It is prohibited to travel more than 2,000 *amos* beyond the limits of a city or town on *Shabbos* or festivals. (There is a great deal of discussion among the commentaries as to whether this prohibition is from the Torah or is rabbinical.) By placing food within 2,000 *amos* of the last home of the city, one can expand the distance that one may travel to a point that is 2,000 *amos* beyond the place where the food was left. The food—the *eruv techumim*—

serves to mix the extended area with the 2,000 *amos* adjoining the town by creating a new point of departure; i.e., the fact that food was left at a point within 2,000 *amos* of the last home in the city serves to extend the city limits to that point.

Eruvin—tractate in the order *Mo'ed.*

Even ha-Ezer—one of the four divisions of *halachah,* which deals with the laws pertaining to the relationships between men and women, first used in the *Tur* of R.Yaakov ben Asher and followed by R.Yosef Caro in his *Shulchan Aruch.*

gaon/geonim—literally, pride; used as a title of respect for a scholar of outstanding erudition. In the period following the sealing of the Talmud, the title was used specifically for the heads of the academies of Sura and Pumbedisa and the various academies in Babylonia that followed their tradition. These Babylonian yeshivos served as a sort of supreme religious authority for all of Jewry, and questions were addressed to them from all over the Jewish world. Most of our information about this period comes from the *Iggeres* of Rav Sherira *Gaon* (see 7.6). The period of the *geonim* began in 500 (4360) and ended in 1038 (4798) with the deaths of R.Shmuel ben Chofni, *Gaon* of Sura, and R. Hai, *Gaon* of Pumbedisa.

gemara—literally, something learned; the Aramaic term used for the Talmudic discussion of the Mishnah.

Gittin—tractate in the order *Nashim.*

halachah—literally, the way; the term is applied to the entire code of Jewish law—both religious and civil.

hashkafah—literally, outlook; the term used to describe the theology of Judaism. It should be noted that while the Rambam included beliefs as an integral part of his *Yad ha-Chazakah* and thus established faith as an integral part of *halachah,* neither the *Tur* nor the *Shulchan Aruch* saw fit to do so.

issur ve-heter—literally, prohibited and permitted; used primarily to describe those parts of *Yoreh De'ah* (see below) that deal with the laws of forbidden foods and mixtures. One who was proficient in these laws and received rabbinic ordination was considered to be capable of ruling in questions of *issur ve-heter.* The use of the term as a description for these laws probably stems from its use in the *Sha'arei Dura* of R. Yitzchak of Dueren (Germany—latter half of the 13th century), subtitled *Isser ve-Hetter shel Rebbi Yitzchak mi-Dura.*

Kesubos—tractate in the order *Nashim.*

Kesuvim—literally, writings; refers to the third of the three divisions of *Tanach,* which includes works written with Divine inspiration rather than prophetic vision.

Kiddushin—tractate in the order *Nashim.*

kinah/kinos—literally, laments; the lamentations composed for recitation in the synagogue on the 9th of *Av.* Through the years additional works were added to commemorate tragedies other than the destruction of the *Beis ha-Mikdash,* including the martyrdom of the Jews of York, the burning of the Talmud in Paris, and the Holocaust.

Kinnim—Mishnaic tractate in the order *Taharos.*

Kodshim—one of the six orders of the Mishnah.

kohen—a descendant of Aharon.

lashon ha-ra—literally, speech that is evil; used to describe the Torah prohibition of slander. The *Chafetz Chaim,* in his masterwork on the subject, notes that one who slanders violates seventeen negative precepts and fourteen positive precepts.

ma'aser/ma'asros—tithes that are required to be separated from produce grown in Eretz Yisrael. There are three forms of *ma'asros. Ma'aser rishon* is given to the Levites for their support. The Levite who receives this portion is required to separate a portion—called *terumas ma'aser*—and give it to a *kohen. Ma'aser sheni* is separated from the produce in the first, second, fourth, and fifth years of the *shemittah* cycle and may be only consumed in Jerusalem in a state of ritual purity (or redeemed for money that is then used to purchase food for consumption). *Ma'aser ani* is given to the poor in the third and sixth years of the *shemittah* cycle.

Makkos—tractate in the order *Nezikin*.

masorah—literally, tradition; used to describe the transmission of the orally received Torah from the time of Moshe onward. The term is also used to describe the manner in which Torah scrolls must be written.

megillos—literally, scrolls; used as a reference to the biblical books *Ruth, Shir ha-Shirim, Koheles, Eichah,* and *Esther.*

Middos—mishnaic tractate in the order *Kodshim.*

Midrash—literally, something that is derived. Although usually used to describe the aggadic exegesis of Scripture, students will also find references to halachic Midrash (see chap. 15).

minhag/minhagim—literally, tradition; used primarily to describe a practice whose source is custom rather than a Torah or rabbinic obligation. It should be noted that once accepted by a community, *minhag* becomes obligatory. For example, the Mishnah (*Bava Basra* 1:1) rules that when partners decide to divide their property, each can insist that the partition used to separate them be constructed of the materials usually used in that area. Neither partner can insist on more expensive or less expensive materials than are usually used. Rabbenu Tam (Tosafos, *Bava Basra* 2a, s.v. *b'gvil*) notes that at times, local custom may be ignored if it is foolish. Many of the laws of separation of a menstruating woman have their basis in *minhag* and have become accepted as halachically binding. R. Shlomo Duran (*Rashbash,* Algiers—1400–1467) notes that *minhag* only has the ability to prohibit something that was permitted, but cannot permit something that was (halachically) prohibited. One of the earliest collections of *minhagim* can be found in the *Sefer ha-Manhig* of R. Avrohom ha-Yarchi (France—1155–1215).

A student of the Ra'avad, he traveled extensively throughout Europe and recorded the *minhagim* practiced in France, England, Germany, and Spain.

Mishnah/mishnayos—literally, teaching; used as a reference to the collection of the halachic statements of the *tanna'im* edited and sealed by R.Yehudah ha-Nasi in 188 (3948). R.Yehudah ha-Nasi did not compose the Mishnah; earlier versions had been compiled by R.Akiva (see *Yerushalmi, Shekalim* 5:1) who lived a century before R.Yehudah ha-Nasi. There is a difference of opinion among the commentators as to whether R.Yehudah ha-Nasi actually committed the Mishnah to writing or only sealed the discussion. R.Saadiah *Gaon* and the Rambam maintain that he did, while Rashi maintains that this was not done until the period of the rabbanan *savora'im*.

misnagdim—literally, opponents; used as a reference to those who opposed the innovations and practices of the followers of R.Yisroel Ba'al Shem Tov and the Maggid of Mezeritch.

Mo'ed—one of the six orders of the Talmud.

moreh tzedek—literally, teacher of righteousness; used as a reference to the recognized halachic authority of a community.

Nashim—one of the six orders of the Talmud.

Nazir—tractate in the order *Nashim*.

Nedarim—tractate in the order *Nashim*.

Nevi'im—literally, prophets; refers to the second of the three divisions of *Tanach* and comprises those works that were written with prophetic vision.

Nezikin—one of the six orders of the Talmud.

Niddah—tractate in the order *Taharos*.

niddah—a woman who has menstruated and has not yet returned to a state of ritual purity by immersing herself in a *mikvah*.

Orach Chaim—one of the four divisions of *halachah,* which deals with ritual law, first used in the *Tur* of R.Yaakov ben Asher and followed by R.Yosef Caro in his *Shulchan Aruch*.

parashah—literally, section; used as a reference to the portion of the Torah read on *Shabbos* in the synagogue. While the practice of reading portions of the Torah each *Shabbos* dates from the time of Moshe, our division of the Torah into 54 *parshios* follows the custom of Babylonia. The original custom in Eretz Yisrael was to divide the Torah into between 153 and 167 *parshios* so that the reading was completed once every three years. We also follow the practice of R. Yehudah in reading the entire *parashah* on *Shabbos* morning rather than dividing it according to the opinion of R. Meir (see *Megillah* 31b). The term *parashah* also refers to the traditional chapter divisions of the Torah, marked in printed editions by the letter פ (פתוחה—open—when the subjects are not related) or ס (סתומה—closed—when the subjects are related). In Torah scrolls, the פתוחה division is created by leaving the space between the last letter and the end of the line empty so that the first verse of the next *parashah* begins on a new line. The סתומה division is created by leaving a space that is the width of nine letters.

parashas Noach—the portion of the Torah comprising the verses from *Bereishis* 6:9 through 11:32.

parashas Vayechi—the portion of the Torah comprising the verses from *Bereishis* 49:1 through 50:26.

Pe'ah—mishnaic tractate in the order *Zerim*.

perek—literally, chapter. The division of *Tanach* into separate chapters that we use today is arbitrary and does not follow the logical sequence of the *parashios* themselves (see entry above). It dates from the thirteenth century and was the work of either Hugo of St. Cher (1200–1263) or Stephen Langton, the Archbishop of Canterbury, who based their divisions on the Latin translation of St. Jerome.

Pesachim—tractate in the order *Mo'ed*.

rabbanan savora'im—literally, the rabbis who applied logic; used as a reference to the rabbis who undertook the final editing of the Talmud *Bavli* in the period between 475 (4235) and 589 (4349).

revi'is—literally, a fourth; a measure of volume equivalent to 0.086 liters (according to R. Chaim Na'eh) or 0.15 liters (according to the *Chazon Ish*).

rishonim—the early masters; i.e., the rabbis and scholars who followed the *geonim*. It is even more difficult to establish a precise date for the beginning of the period of the *rishonim* than for the *acharonim*, for there is a longer overlapping period between the two eras. R. Hai and Rabbenu Gershom were contemporaries, yet the former unquestionably belongs to the period of the *geonim* whereas the latter is unquestionably a *rishon*. Generally, we can state that the period of the *rishonim* began with the decline in importance of the academies of Babylonia around the year 1000 and the concurrent rise in influence of the Jewish communities of North Africa and Europe.

rosh yeshivah—dean of a talmudic academy.

Seder/Sedarim—literally, order; used as a reference to the traditional division of the Talmud into six sections of varying lengths. This divison is mentioned in the Talmud (see *Bava Metzia* 85b).

Sephard—literally, Spain; used as a reference to the Jewish communities of Spain and North Africa, and later to those of the Near East as well. The traditions of Sephardic Jewry are based primarily on the rulings of the Rambam and the Rif as brought by R. Yosef Caro. It would seem that these communities introduced fewer changes in the traditions handed down from the *geonim* than did the communities of northern Europe, though there are some differences between the customs of North African Jewry and Near Eastern Jewry. The term is also used to describe the text of the prayers introduced by the *Ari ha-Kadosh*.

Shekalim—tractate in the order *Mo'ed*.

shemittah—the Sabbatical year.

sidrah—literally, order; used as a synonym for *parashah* when referring to the weekly Torah portion.

Taharos—one of the six orders of the Talmud.

takkanos—literally, repairs; used as a reference for ordinances enacted by a halachic authority or by the community. A *takkanah* differs from pure *halachah* in that it is not based on a scriptural or logical derivation, but rather on the perception that the enactment is required for the public's welfare. Thus, a *takkanah* is a rabbinical obligation (although the obligation to follow the *takkanah* is, according to some commentators, a Torah requirement). Although rabbinical in origin, a *takkanah* has the ability to overule a positive Torah precept in the sense that the authorities can decide to cancel the requirement to fulfill the latter in a given situation. For example, though the Torah requires one to sound the *shofar* on Rosh Hashannah, the rabbis decreed that this should not be done if the holiday falls on *Shabbos* (see *Rosh Hashanah* 29b). Similarly, Hillel's enactment of the *prozbul,* whereby one can transfer debts owed him to the court and thus collect during the *shemittah* year, is also an example of the power of *takkanah* to contravene a Torah law (see *Shevi'is* 10:3–4). The source of the authority to enact binding *takkanos* is the subject of a dispute between the Rambam (*Sefer ha-Mitzvos, Shoresh* I) and the Ramban (ad loc.).

tanna/tanna'im—literally, those who teach; used as a reference to the rabbis and sages whose statements are quoted in the Mishnah. The period of the *tanna'im* began with Hillel and Shammai (first century B.C.E.) and ended with the redaction of the Mishnah by R. Yehudah ha-Nasi in 188. *Tanna'im* have more authority than *ammora'im* in that they are considered to be capable of offering their own exegesis (both logical and scriptural—see Part IV).

techiyas ha-meisim—resurrection of the dead; a principal belief of Judaism according to the thirteen principles outlined by the Rambam (Commentary to the Mishnah, *Sanhedrin* 11:1).

Temurah—tractate in the order *Kodshim.*

terumah/terumos—literally, donation; the portion of produce that one is required to separate in the Land of Israel and give to a *kohen* as a means for his support.

Tishah b'Av—the 9th of *Av,* the day declared as a fast in commemoration of the destruction of the first and second *Batei Mikdash.*

tosefta—literally, an addition; used as a synonym for *beraisa* but also including tannaitic statements that are not included in the Talmud.

tzara'as—a spiritual disease whose physical manifestations are the same as leprosy.

Yoreh De'ah—one of the four divisions of *halachah,* which deals with ritual law, first used in the *Tur* of R.Yaakov ben Asher and followed by R.Yosef Caro in his *Shulchan Aruch.*

Zera'im—one of the six orders of the Talmud.

Selected Bibliography

The following reference works have been helpful, and students might find it worthwhile to peruse them to deepen their appreciation and understanding of the issues touched upon. It should be noted that many students overlook the most important source for material—the introductions and prefaces of many *seforim,* which usually explain the author's reasons for writing his work. They are also an invaluable source for biographical and historical material.

ספרים בעברית:

אורבך, אפרים. בעלי התוספות מוסד ביאליק, ירושלים, 5728.

אזולאי, הרב יוסף חיים דוד. שם הגדולים. וורשא, 5636.

אייזענשטיין, יהודה דוד. אוצר ישראל ספר, ירושלים.

אינצקלופדיה תלמודית. ירושלים, 5727.

אסף, שמחה. תקופת הגאונים וספרותה. ירושלים, 5715.

הלוי, יצחק אייזק. דורות ראשונים. מפעלי ספרים ליצוא. ירושלים.

הלפרין, רפאל. אטלס עץ חיים הקדש רוח יעקב. 5745.

יעב"ץ, זאב. תולדות ישראל. לונדון, 5682.

מרגליות, מרדכי. אינצקלופדיה לתולדות גדולי ישראל. צ׳יצ׳יק, תל אביב, 5710.

פדר, י. שמעון. תולדות הדורות סמינר באר יעקב, 5743.

רוטנברג, שלמה. תולדות עם עולם. קרן אליעזר, ברוקלין, 5744.

שפוטץ, דוד. שנות דוד ודור. ברוקלין, 5740.

English works:

Encyclopædia Judaica. Jerusalem: Keter Publishing, 1972.

Fendel, Zechariah. *Masters of the Mesorah,* vols. 1 and 2. New York: Hashkafah Publications, 1990.

Holder, Meir. *History of the Jewish People—From Yavneh to Pumbedisah.* New York: Mesorah Publications, 1986.

Waxman, Meir. *A History of Jewish Literature,* vols. 1–5. New York: Bloch Publishing, 1938.

Index of Names

Index of Works

Subject Index

About the Author

Born and raised in McKeesport, Pennsylvania, Dovid Landesman made *aliyah* in 1972. A graduate of Mesifta Torah Vodaath in Brooklyn and Yeshivas Beis ha-Talmud in Jerusalem, he holds a B.A. from Queens College and an M.S. from Long Island University. A translator and editor in both Hebrew and English, he recently published *Rinah shel Torah*—The Commentary of the *Netziv* to *Shir ha-Shirim*— and is currently at work on a new English translation and commentary to *Ein Yaakov*. He also teaches Talmud and *Navi* at Midreshet ha-Galil, a yeshivah high school for gifted Russian students in Migdal ha-Emek. He and his wife, Nechama, reside in Kfar Chassidim, Israel, with their eight children.